Dedicated to my grandmother Veronica
who passed away in 2010.
She lives in me.

Eating

for the

Seasons

Cooking for health and happiness

JANELLA PURCELL

ALLEN&UNWIN

First published by Allen & Unwin in 2011
Copyright © 2011 Janella Purcell

Allen & Unwin
83 Alexander Street
Crows Nest NSW 2065
Australia
Phone: (61 2) 8425 0100
Fax: (61 2) 9906 2218
Email: info@allenandunwin.com
Web: www.allenandunwin.com

Cataloguing-in-Publication details are available from the National Library of Australia
www.trove.nla.gov.au

ISBN: 978 1 74175 408 7

Design: Emily O'Neill
Food stylist: Jody Vassallo
Photographer: Billy Wrencher
Home economist: Amelia Hamilton

The author and publisher would like to thank the following for their generous help:
Melrose Foods
Heart Breads, Byron Bay
The Bay Seafood Market, Byron Bay
Mud Australia
Heath's Old Wares

Colour reproduction by Splitting Image, Clayton, Victoria
Printed in China by South China Printing Co.

10 9 8 7 6 5 4

Contents

To all things
in moderation
including
moderation!

Introduction

Growing up with a Lebanese mother, you can well imagine how food, cooking and eating were an integral part of my childhood. As a young girl I learnt to cook at my grandmother and mother's knees, making their traditional dishes.

It was generally a healthy diet, in moderation, but I struggled with my health and weight. Certain foods definitely did not agree with my body, but I wasn't sure what I should eat instead.

In my twenties I decided to study naturopathy and nutrition to find out what was going on. Through extensive reading, I became aware that different foods have different kinds of energy. Some foods move energy up and out, others down and in. These discoveries led me to an ongoing study of Traditional Chinese Medicine. Thousands of years old, this ancient discipline talks about why we should eat food when it is in season and the effects that food and our emotions have on different organs in our bodies. This explained so much to me, and the jigsaw puzzle started to come together.

But it's not all about the food. It's also the amount eaten and the time of day it is consumed, as well as the mood you are in when you eat. As I developed a more wholistic approach to health, the notion of balance in other areas of my life—getting appropriate exercise, having enough sleep and clean water, understanding my emotions, knowing what my needs were and how to get them met and, most importantly, knowing and accepting my worth—also became important. Essentially, it was about living a balanced life.

Living in balance forms the basis of the Japanese macrobiotic diet; a diet that also shows us the importance of eating food that naturally grows around us. This knowledge is now being recognised in the west and its wisdoms are evident in the way we are changing our habits. We're becoming more hands-on with our food. Many of us have vegie patches in our backyards and we are shopping more often at grower's markets, where the produce is straight from the farms and in season. It is clear at these markets that we have no need, for example, to eat watermelon in winter due to its lack of availability, and the farmers can offer us first-hand advice about their harvests.

I now knew what to eat, when, how and why. I was excited to realise that what I'd learnt on my journey was of value to others and so I wrote my first book, *Elixir*, showing how to use the food you eat as medicine. The feedback I receive from readers is so encouraging. Many are keen to learn more about food as medicine, and the interconnectedness of the body, mind and spirit. A recipe book was the obvious next step.

It gives me so much pleasure to share what I've learnt thus far in *Eating for the Seasons*. To know how to properly nourish and nurture yourself and the ones you love will be one of the most empowering things you will ever learn. Welcome to a healthy relationship with food. This is where it begins.

Janella Purcell

Janella's principles of good food

Eating seasonally gives your body the food it needs, as that's what is growing around you. Nature knows, for example, that in summer you don't really want or need a heavy meal; instead, if you're listening, you'll lean towards light food that is either mostly raw or has been quickly cooked. And in the cooler months, coming home to a bowl of salad isn't that appealing. If you ignore your body's needs, symptoms will result to let you know that something is not quite right.

Eating for the Seasons is based on Asian principles. I've made sure that in each season of the year, you'll find delicious, nutritious and healthy foods for every part of the day. And best of all, this food is easy to prepare.

For every season there is an object, an organ that is most sensitive and a different emotion that will be associated with that time of year. It's important to be aware of this, as it will help you work out why you're feeling the way you do or why at the same time every year you get the same symptoms. For example, in spring you may get headaches and feel angry, in summer sluggish and worried, in autumn you may suffer chest infections and feel sad, and in winter you may be inclined towards urinary tract infections and feel isolated, alone and anxious. By eating what you need you're giving you body, mind and spirit the best chance at balance.

You'll notice that there are no recipes for red or white meat in my book. I don't eat red or white meat but, if you do, I've made simple suggestions for varying some of the recipes. Once you feel comfortable with eating to nurture your body, you'll feel confident to add new ingredients you may not have used before and remain mindful of the principles of healthy eating.

When selecting ingredients to cook, make sure they are the real thing. For instance, maple syrup may not be maple syrup but an imitation. If possible, select organic or biodynamic foods over intensively-farmed produce. They're better for you, and there is no substitute for good quality produce. I also only use filtered water in my recipes, and I recommend this to my clients.

Some of the ingredients I've used in the recipes may be harder to find than the usual choices but they're worth taking the time to locate. There are some handy starting places on where to find ingredients in the glossary. Don't be put off using something just because you haven't used it before. The ingredients are usually quick and easy to prepare and cook and the method is outlined in the recipe. For grains, see the box opposite for cooking advice.

How to cook grains

The amount of water, cooking time and number of serves below are for 1 cup of raw ingredients.

Grain	Water	Cooking Time	Serves
Amaranth	Double	30 mins	4 to 6
Barley	2½ times	35–40 mins	4 to 6
Buckwheat	Double	15–25 mins	4 to 6
Bulghar	Double	Pour over boiling water, cover and set aside for 15 mins	4 to 6
Couscous	Double	Pour over boiling water, cover and set aside for 15 mins	4 to 6
Freekeh	2½ times	30–40 mins	4 to 6
Millet	2½ to 3 times	30–45 mins	4 to 6
Oat flakes	2½ to 3 times	15–30 mins	2 to 3
Polenta	3 to 3½ times	15–20 mins	4 to 6
Quinoa	Double	15 mins	4
Rice, white	Double	20–35 mis	4 to 6
Rice, brown	2 to 2½ times	35–45 mins	4
Rye grains	3½ times	90 mins	4
Wheat grains	4½ times	45–60 mins	4 to 6

Recipe codes

Dairy-free	[df]	Vegan	[vg]
Gluten-free	[gf]	Vegetarian	[v]

Your year-round pantry

Below are items I suggest you keep in your refrigerator, cupboard, freezer or under your bench. As each season produces its own abundance of fresh foods, I've listed what's good for that time of year in the opening spreads of each season.

Keep in the fridge

Hummus
Goat's cheese
Yoghurt
Fish sauce

Tofu: firm, silken and smoked, marinated
Fresh herbs: parsley, coriander, mint, basil, spring onions
Smoked trout

Keep in the cupboard

Organic brown rice
Quinoa
Freekeh
Millet
Amaranth
Oats
Muesli
Spelt flakes
Spelt bread
Anchovies
Mountain bread
Canned legumes
Spelt crackers
Baked corn chips
Shiitake mushrooms
Dashi
Kombu
Arame
Miso paste
Tahini, hulled
Olive oil
Sesame oil

Spelt flour
Balsamic vinegar
Sweeteners like raw honey, rice syrup, agave syrup, pear and/or apple juice concentrate, maple syrup
Sea salt
Spices: turmeric, cumin seeds, garam masala, coriander seeds, chilli, black and white peppercorns
Dark chocolate
Dried fruit
Roasted mixed nuts
Sesame seeds
Sunflower seeds
LSA
Pepitas
Tamari (soy sauce)
Soup mix
Instant miso soup
Vanilla pod
Herbal teas
Milk—soy, rice and almond

Keep in the freezer

Stock
Your bag of leftovers and scraps ready
    for making stock

Berries
Fish fillets and whole fish
Green prawns

Making stock

Most commercially available stocks are heavy in salt and sugar, and I think they make all your dishes taste the same. I get enormous satisfaction from opening the freezer and seeing all those neatly stacked containers full of my stock. So this is how I do it.

When you're preparing your vegies—topping and tailing, peeling them (although this should be rare), taking the skins off garlic and ginger, trimming your broccoli—don't throw these scraps away. Instead, put them in a plastic bag in the freezer. Don't throw any scraps out. I even use the stalks of herbs, peas shells, celery leaves—the lot! I don't use beetroot skins or red cabbage scraps (they make the stock red) or potato skins (too dirty). On that note, if your vegies do have a bit of dirt on them, then wipe it off. Of course, throw in any vegies that are past their best that you might normally throw away.

I also freeze prawn shells, fish frames, and any offcuts when I'm preparing seafood. Keep filling the bags until you have enough to make your stock. I tend to have quite a few big bags of scraps in my freezer.

When you're ready to make the stock, empty the bags into a large stockpot and cover it with filtered water. Bring it to the boil, and then drop it to a simmer for about 45 minutes, giving it a stir occasionally. Be sure to have your exhaust on and open your windows as it does have quite a strong fragrance. After it has cooled slightly, take the pot over to the sink. Drain the stock through a colander into a big bowl. Then transfer the clear liquid into containers and stack them in the freezer.

You can make one stock from vegies and another from organic chicken or red meat bones and leftover flesh. It's a nice way to use every part of the animal and minimise waste. The leftover pulps (if using only vegies) can then go into your compost or worm farm.

You won't believe how much better your food tastes when you take the time to make your own stock and how good you feel knowing you're not wasting anything.

Spring

By the time spring arrives, most of us are ready to *farewell the winter*. Springtime reminds us of our youth, of renewal and beginnings. This is why spring is acknowledged as the first season of the year. We have experienced the seasons in full circle and are now back at the start. When you look at *rocket*, *asparagus* or *parsley*, you can see that it grows up and outwards. This is exactly what our energy does in springtime. It moves *'up and out'*.

Object

It's time to renew your energy. With the warmer months after the cold of winter you will begin to feel lighter, emotionally and physically, and the food you desire should be lighter as well.

Spring prompts you to get outside, to play, socialise and have fun—all those things you did when you were a kid. That also means you'll want to spend less time in the kitchen. Who wants to spend hours indoors in the heat of the kitchen when the sun is shining outside?

Organ

Your liver and gallbladder will be sensitive now. The liver is the main organ for detoxification—that's why so many of us tend to cut down our intake of alcohol, fats, oil and junk food during spring.

Emotion

The emotions stored in the liver are anger, resentment, irritability, frustration, impatience, depression and indecisiveness.

Symptoms

Digestive complaints, especially nausea, allergies, eye and skin problems, neck and back tension, fingernail or toenail problems, and reproductive issues may arise. Chronic indigestion and fatigue, an inflexible body, muscular pain, tendon problems and you may find that you're slow to get going in the morning.

Flavour & foods

- Sour is the flavour that stimulates the liver and gallbladder. Sour flavours are things like lemons and limes.

- Sweet flavours are also recommended in spring; foods like complex carbohydrates and sweeteners. Complex carbohydrates include foods like fruits and vegetables, whole grains, legumes, nuts and seeds. By sweeteners I mean complex sweeteners like rice syrup, real maple syrup, spelt syrup, agave and raw honey.
- Bitter foods are also encouraged; things like rocket, rye, radicchio and chamomile.
- It's the weather to eat young greens and fast-growing plants like salad greens, sprouts, wheat grass and barley greens.
- Fruit salad and juices are recommended.
- Cabbage, broccoli and dark leafy greens will be of benefit here as they promote the digestion of meat—usually we eat more meat throughout winter so these foods help us move on from that season.
- This is the time for scallops, prawns and calamari as opposed to fish. This doesn't mean you need to avoid fish; it just means that other kinds of seafood are recommended now.
- Enjoy herbs like mint, basil, fennel, rosemary, dill and bay leaf.

Cooking methods

Cook at high temperatures for shorter times, with less water and salt, so your vegetables are still crunchy—stir-fry or steam, for example, or make leafy green salads with sprouts, legumes, lemon zest and herbs.

Avoid

In winter we usually eat more salty foods like meat, cheese, soy sauce, nuts and fast food. These now need to be reduced. Too much heavy food will put a big strain on your liver, as will excessive amounts of alcohol.

Fresh in spring

Fruit: apple / cumquat / grapefruit / lemon / mandarin / orange / papaya / paw paw / pineapple / tangelo / avocado / broad star fruit / tomato

Vegetables: watercress / silver beet / spinach / lettuce / artichoke / bok choy / choy sum / asparagus (green and purple) / green bean / cabbage / carrot / cauliflower / garlic / ginger / leek / mushroom / green pea / pumpkin / sweetcorn / zucchini flower / beetroot

Seafood: Atlantic salmon / coral trout / long-fin eel / ocean jacket / Spanish mackerel / snapper / tuna / abalone / spanner crab / eastern rock lobster

Breakfast

1 FREE-RANGE EGG
1 TSP MIRIN (*optional*)
½ TSP WHITE PEPPER
1 TSP OLIVE OIL
1 PC MOUNTAIN BREAD

1 TBSP SOFT GOAT'S CHEESE
SMALL HANDFUL BABY SPINACH,
ROCKET OR KALE
½ TSP TAMARI

One egg omelette *in* mountain bread [v]

This has become one of my favourite things to eat. I recommend it to so many people and they all agree it's a perfect breakfast. Wrap it in the thin flat bread and you won't be hungry until lunchtime. Mirin is a Japanese sherry commonly used in sauces and stir-fries and it adds flavour.

SERVES 1

Whisk egg with mirin and pepper until fluffy. Heat a flat, non-stick pan and add the oil and heat. Pour in the egg and swirl around so it looks like a crepe. Cook for about 30 seconds, then flip. Scrape the cheese on to the bread then top with the egg. Add the greens then drizzle with the Tamari.

Variations

- Use flaked smoked trout, cooked fish, crab meat or two to three cooked prawns, peeled, de-veined and sliced in half widthwise.
- Try feta and sautéed garlic mushrooms instead of goat's cheese.
- Add lots of chopped herbs like parsley, mint and/or coriander to your wrap.
- Add pan-fried smoked or marinated tofu to your wrap for an extra hit of protein.
- Stir-fry a bit of garlic and spring onion in the pan before the egg goes in.
- Add a teaspoon of raw honey to the Tamari for a sweeter sauce.
- Use avocado instead of goat's cheese.
- After the egg comes out of the pan, turn off the heat and toss in a handful of chopped kale or silverbeet. Add this to the wrap in cooler months instead of the raw greens.

1 CUP RICE MILK

½ CUP FROZEN FRUIT LIKE MIXED BERRIES

1–2 TSP SWEETENER SUCH AS RICE SYRUP, PEAR/APPLE CONCENTRATE, RAW HONEY OR AGAVE SYRUP

2 TSP LECITHIN

1 TSP PSYLLIUM HUSKS

1 TSP SPIRULINA POWDER (*optional*)

Smoothie [*df, gf, vg, v*]

Almost everyone loves a smoothie. You can experiment with it all you like. I usually recommend it to my clients (or myself) when trying to shed a few kilos. In this case add the psyllium husks as they act as an appetite suppressant due to the way they bulk up in the digestive tract. Be sure to drink lots of water afterwards, otherwise you might find it difficult to digest the husks. The lecithin helps process fat through the liver and soaks up bad cholesterol. It also has a nice little crunch to it. The spirulina will make your smoothie green, although it won't change the taste too much. It's worth adding (add a little bit at first if you're not sure) as it's so good for you. Spirulina is a complete food, meaning it contains all 22 amino acids so it's very high in protein and is a great way to start the day. It's also wonderful for helping cool the liver and deal with fat.

SERVES 1

Pop all the ingredients into a blender and combine well.
Serve in a tall glass.

Variations

- Rice milk is very thin in consistency and low in fat, something like skim milk, but sweeter. Almond milk may be substituted if you like a richer smoothie, and it's high in calcium and good fat. Or try oat, hazlenut or quinoa milk. Stick with the rice milk if you're on a mission to lose weight, though.
- Mix in a tablespoon of Breakfast Booster (by Melrose Foods) instead of the last three ingredients.
- Add a tablespoon of LSA (linseed, sunflower and almond mix) for extra crunch and a massive nutrient boost.
- A tablespoon of flaxseed oil thrown in is great for its weight-loss, anti-inflammatory and other health-giving properties.
- Half a cup of muesli—raw or toasted—is a good addition.
- Avoid using ice as it will slow down your metabolism due to messing up digestive juices. If you really miss having it cold, then freeze your fruit first or buy it already frozen.

Spirulina is high in protein, as is amaranth.

2 TBSP OLIVE OIL

8 FREE-RANGE EGGS

1 CUP GOAT'S FETA, CRUMBLED

HANDFUL MINT LEAVES, SHREDDED

CRACKED PEPPER

Scrambled eggs *with* feta *and* mint [*gf, v*]

Here's a quick, tasty, protein-packed, creamy breakfast. Try using goat's feta instead of cow's. It has a stronger taste but is anti-inflammatory and lower in fat than cheese made from cow's milk. And please use the whole egg, not just the white. Eggs provide wonderful protein and recent research has shown that eggs in moderation won't raise your cholesterol.

SERVES 4

Add oil to a flat pan—a non-stick pan will make life easy.
Beat the eggs until fluffy then add the feta, mint and pepper.
Pour this mixture into the pan and gently fold the eggs as they cook. Lovely just like this or wrapped inside mountain bread.

Variations

- Add crushed garlic with the oil, which is my preference, although it's not everyone's idea of morning food.
- Use four spring onions, adding the white parts with the olive oil, and using the green tops as a garnish. You could also add one to two cloves of garlic with the spring onion.
- Sauté sliced mushrooms and/or corn kernels with garlic in the oil before adding the eggs.
- Wrap the eggs in mountain bread with some baby spinach then toast in a sandwich press.

Include more sour foods in your diet during spring as this is the time to take extra-special care of your liver. Lemon juice in a little warm water, first thing in the morning, will kick start your liver.

Lunch

---

6 CUPS WATERMELON, CUT INTO
BIG CHUNKS

2 CUPS GOAT'S FETA, CUT INTO 3-CM
CUBES

4 TBSP OLIVE OIL

2 TBSP GOOD BALSAMIC VINEGAR

SEA SALT AND CRACKED PEPPER

TWO HANDFULS WATERCRESS

Watermelon, feta *and* watercress salad [*gf, v*]

Watermelon is a cooling food and perfect for the warmer weather. Its flavour is sweet and its colour screams the season. I know this combination of watermelon and feta may sound odd but I guarantee, once tasted, you'll make it often.

SERVES 4

This salad is 'layered'. Place a few chunks of watermelon on each of your serving plates, and top with some feta. Combine the oil, vinegar and seasoning and drizzle some of the mixture over each of the watermelon and feta mounds. Top the salads with a generous handful of watercress, and then finish with a little more of the oil, and vinegar and pepper.

Variations

- Use marinated feta instead—there are some wonderful combinations out there.
- Add torn mint leaves with or without the watercress.
- Add blood orange segments with the watermelon—it adds a whole other dimension.

2 SMALL PKTS BEAN THREAD
VERMICELLI

½ CUP TAMARI

½ TSP SESAME OIL

1 PKT SMALL ROUND RICE PAPER
WRAPPERS

2 SHEETS NORI, CUT INTO THICK
MATCHSTICKS

2 CARROTS, JULIENNED

1 LEBANESE CUCUMBER, SKIN ON
AND JULIENNED

2 AVOCADOS, SLICED

3 CUPS YUMMY TOFU (*see page 154*)

8 SPRING ONIONS, SLICED DIAGONALLY

1 CUP EACH MINT AND CORIANDER
LEAVES

Fresh spring rolls [*df, gf, vg, v*]

Rice wrappers are a blessing when you're first learning to live without wheat. For a light, fresh and tasty lunch with good friends, serve all the ingredients on a platter and roll as you go. These are the fillings I use most often but you should experiment with your preferred fillings. Nori is a dried sea vegetable available in paper-thin sheets that you can eat as a snack or wrap around rice. It has a high protein and iodine content and is the most easily digested of the seaweeds.

SERVES 4

Place the noodles in a bowl and cover with hot water. They will soften in a few minutes.

Meanwhile, combine the Tamari and sesame oil and pour into small, individual bowls, one for each person. Place the rest of the ingredients in piles around the edges of a large serving platter with the herbs in the middle. Strain the noodles and place on the serving platter.

To serve, put the platter in the middle of the table and have a ceramic bowl of boiling water on the table. Each person places their own rice paper wrapper in the water for about 15 seconds then gently removes it and puts it on their plate. Place a piece of nori in the centre of the rice paper and then add a couple of pieces of carrot, a piece each of cucumber and avocado, and top with a piece of Yummy Tofu and a small amount of noodles and spring onions. Finish with a sprinkling of coriander and mint—don't fill the wraps too much, as they might burst when rolling or eating. Roll up by folding over the end closest to you, tucking in the outer edges and continuing to roll. They will stick together so is no need to add water to secure them. Eat with the dipping sauce.

Variations

- Mix one teaspoon rice wine vinegar and/or one teaspoon grated coconut palm sugar with the cucumber.
- Use sliced garlic prawns or shredded organic chicken instead of or as well as the tofu.

1 KG (2 lb 2 oz) CLAMS

1 CUP QUINOA GRAINS

2 TBSP SPRING ONIONS, WHITE PARTS ONLY, FINELY CHOPPED

2 CLOVES GARLIC, CRUSHED

1 TBSP CORIANDER STEMS, FINELY CHOPPED

2 ANCHOVIES

2 TBSP OLIVE OIL

½ CUP WHITE WINE

1–2 TSP CHILLI FLAKES OR FRESH, CHOPPED, OR TO TASTE

½ CUP ITALIAN PARSLEY, ROUGHLY CHOPPED

CRACKED PEPPER

1 LEMON CUT INTO WEDGES, TO SERVE

Clams *with* quinoa [*df, gf*]

This is one of my favourite dishes. I like to have it for Sunday lunch served with a big green salad. Quinoa is a plant that grows at high altitudes. These small seeds, from a herb rather than a grain, are gluten-free, rich in vitamins and nutrients and were much prized by the Incas. If you prefer noodles, I often serve the vongole and its luscious juices with quinoa udon.

SERVES 4

Leave the clams in the fridge covered with a wet tea towel while preparing the dish. Don't wash them as this will dilute their flavour.

Cook the quinoa (*see 'How to cook grains' on page 3*), then set aside. Next, chop together the spring onions, garlic, coriander and anchovies to form a chunky paste.

In a nice big pot heat the oil then add the paste. Quickly sauté, then add the clams and wine and stir. Put the lid on and shake the pan a few times to mix everything together. Leave on a low heat for about one minute, giving the pan a shake every so often. The clams will open up—the ones that don't open need to be discarded.

Stir in the cooked quinoa, then finish with the chilli and plenty of parsley and cracked pepper. Taste, as you may want to add some sea salt but the clams are so salty that it's not usually necessary. Serve with lemon wedges.

Variations

- Mussels are lovely also, just leave out the coriander and add teaspoon of dried or fresh thyme.
- Use quinoa udon instead of grains.
- Leave out the coriander stems and add basil with the parsley.

1 PKT QUINOA UDON OR
SPELT SPAGHETTI

1 ONION, DICED

2–4 GARLIC CLOVES, CRUSHED

2 ANCHOVIES (*optional but recommended*)

1–2 TSP SEA SALT

8 GREEN PRAWNS, SHELLED AND
CLEANED

8 SCALLOPS

200 G (7 oz) CALAMARI RINGS

1 PIECE WHITE FISH LIKE FLATHEAD,
BARRAMUNDI OR SNAPPER,
CHOPPED INTO 2-CM PIECES

8 MUSSELS

½ CUP OLIVE OIL

GOOD SPLASH WHITE WINE

½ CUP EACH ITALIAN PARSLEY AND
BASIL, ROUGHLY CHOPPED

CRACKED PEPPER

Seafood marinara [*df*]

Spring is the time to enjoy seafood like calamari, prawns, clams and vongole. Put them all together to make this heavenly pasta, or for a lovely bouillabaisse add red wine, more stock and tomato sauce and maybe a crab claw or four. Serve in a bowl with a bib and prepare to get messy.

SERVES 4

Cook the noodles according to manufacturer's instructions. Pound in a mortar and pestle or chop together the onions, garlic and anchovies with a little of the anchovy (or use olive) oil and 1 tsp salt. Put all the seafood in a bowl and rub the garlic mixture through. Add a little more oil if needed to help the garlic coat the seafood.

In a flat pan or wok, cook the seafood separately—you shouldn't need to add more oil, especially if you use a non-stick pan, but do if you need to. Cook each type until almost done and remove from pan. Now, place all the seafood back in the pan. Add the wine, and let it simmer for a few seconds to let the alcohol reduce. Now gently mix through the noodles. Finally, toss in the parsley and basil then taste for seasoning—add as much or as little as you need.

Variations

- Stir through half a cup of napoli sauce (*see page 180*), one cup of roughly chopped fresh tomatoes, or half a can of chopped tomatoes just after adding the wine.
- Add chilli flakes or chilli jam with the wine if you'd like some heat.

Dressing

2 TBSP EXTRA VIRGIN OLIVE OIL

1 TBSP WHITE BALSAMIC VINEGAR

½ TBSP RAW HONEY

½ TBSP DIJON MUSTARD

1 LEMON, JUICED

½ TSP SEA SALT

1 FENNEL BULB

1 CUP MINT LEAVES, ROUGHLY CHOPPED

½ CUP ITALIAN PARSLEY, ROUGHLY CHOPPED

3 CUPS SMOKED TROUT

A FEW SPRIGS CHERVIL, FOR GARNISH (optional)

Smoked trout *and* fennel salad [df, gf]

These flavours go perfectly together. It's a quick salad to prepare so you'll probably make it a lot. Add tomato and feta for a bigger, more complex salad in spring, while it's still a little cool.

SERVES 4

For the dressing, place all the ingredients into a bottle with a lid. Shake until combined.

Trim any dark bits off the fennel, and then trim the green leafy parts off the top. Chop the green leafy parts and mix with the mint and parsley. Finely shave the remaining fennel bulb with a peeler, mandolin or knife. Place a little of the fennel on the bottom of a platter and drizzle with a little dressing. Sprinkle over a little of the herbs and fennel tops. Then add a layer of trout and drizzle again with the dressing and herbs. Finish with a layer of fennel, herbs and dressing. Garnish with chervil (if using).

Variations

- Dot goat's feta and/or cherry tomatoes around the layers on the plate.
- Add sliced avocado to the salad.
- Add one clove crushed garlic to the dressing.

1–2 TBSP OLIVE OIL

2 SPRING ONIONS, FINELY CHOPPED

2 GARLIC CLOVES, CRUSHED

1–2 TSP CHILLI, FRESH OR FLAKES
(OR TO TASTE)

1 BUNCH BROCCOLINI, TRIMMED

1 PKT SPELT SPAGHETTI OR
QUINOA UDON

2 CUPS SMOKED TROUT

1 TBSP LEMON ZEST

1 TBSP CAPERS

1 CUP MINT AND PARSLEY,
FINELY CHOPPED

CRACKED PEPPER

LEMON JUICE AND OLIVE OIL,
TO GARNISH

Smoked trout, broccolini *and* lemon pasta [*df*]

Eating pasta is fine as long as it's not made from refined wheat and you avoid creamy, fatty sauces. It's better to eat pasta at lunchtime and then go for a big walk afterwards. If you're trying to lose weight then avoid pasta and noodles for a while.

SERVES 4

Heat the olive oil in a shallow pan, add the spring onion and sauté. Add the garlic and chilli and cook gently for a minute then remove from the heat.

Meanwhile bring a pot of water to the boil. Place the broccolini in the pot and blanch for about 30 seconds, keeping it green. Scoop out with a slotted spoon and refresh broccolini under cold water to stop it cooking further. Set aside.

Next, place the pasta in the boiling water and cook until al dente, then strain.

Place the pan back on the heat and flake the trout into the pan with the lemon zest and capers. Stir to combine. Toss in the pasta and broccolini then finish with lots of herbs and seasoning. Drizzle with lemon juice and extra olive oil.

Variation

- Use green peas instead of the broccolini.

2 BUNCHES ASPARAGUS, ENDS SNAPPED
OFF AND STALKS CUT INTO THIRDS

1 CAULIFLOWER, CUT INTO FLORETS

2 CANS WHITE BEANS, LIKE CANNELLINI
OR LIMA BEANS

1 CUP ROASTED WALNUTS

HANDFUL MINT, CHOPPED

2 TBSP WALNUT OR OLIVE OIL

1 TBSP WHITE BALSAMIC OR
RASPBERRY VINEGAR

SEA SALT

Asparagus, cauliflower *and* white bean salad [*df, gf, vg, v*]

Canned legumes are handy to have in the pantry. Just be sure to get a brand that has no added salt or sugar and, if possible, get one that has cooked the beans with kombu. Kombu is a seaweed that contains 500 times the iodine of shellfish. High in protein, iron and calcium, it's great in soups, salads, bean dishes and pickles. Of course, feel free to cook your own—just remember to add a stick of Kombu to the pot when they're cooking.

SERVES 4 AS A SIDE

Blanch asparagus and cauliflower in simmering water until just tender—it should take around three minutes—then refresh under cold water. Combine the vegies, beans, walnuts and mint in a bowl and toss gently. For the dressing, put the oil and vinegar in a jar and season; shake well. Dress the salad and gently toss again. Taste for seasoning.

Variations

- Add one teaspoon of shiro miso to the dressing for a creamier mixture.
- Almost any salad is lifted by adding a little grated lemon or lime zest to the dressing.
- Serve Tahini Dressing (*see page 149*) on the side so it can be added as required.

In spring it's best to eat more raw foods than you would throughout winter. That doesn't mean go on a raw-food diet; it means be conscious of not having to cook everything all the way through.

4 CUPS VEGETABLE OR FISH STOCK

1 TBSP TAMARI

2 TBSP ARAME

1 TBSP APPLE JUICE CONCENTRATE

1 TBSP MIRIN

1 TBSP GINGER, GRATED

1 CUP BAMBOO SHOOTS, SLICED

2 CARROTS, JULIENNED

2 CUPS FRESH SHIITAKE MUSHROOMS, SLICED

2 CUPS BROCCOLI FLORETS OR BROCCOLINI, TRIMMED AND CUT IN HALF

1 BUNCH ASIAN GREENS LIKE CHOY SUM OR BOK CHOY

1 PKT JAPANESE NOODLES MADE FROM QUINOA, BUCKWHEAT OR BROWN RICE, COOKED, DRAINED AND RINSED

2 TBSP GOMASHIO, TO GARNISH (*optional*)

2 TBSP SPRING ONION, FINELY CHOPPED, TO GARNISH

1 CUP CORIANDER LEAVES, TO GARNISH

1 CUP BEAN SPROUTS, TO GARNISH

Japanese broth *with* udon noodles [*df, gf*]

This is a simple, clear and nourishing soup. Perfect if you're feeling stressed and don't have much of an appetite—in this case use quinoa grains instead of noodles. Arame is a seaweed containing ten times the calcium of milk and 500 times the iodine of shellfish, so is extra good for you.

SERVES 4

Pop the first six ingredients in a soup pot and bring to a steady simmer. Then add the bamboo shoots, carrots, mushrooms and broccoli and cook until just tender, about two minutes. Turn off the heat and add the Asian greens, just allowing them to wilt.

To serve, divide the noodles between four soup bowls, then cover with the vegetables and broth. Garnish with gomashio, spring onions, coriander leaves and bean sprouts.

Variations

- Use three sachets of dashi dissolved in a litre of filtered water instead of stock for a deeper and saltier Asian flavor.
- Add more vegetables if you like, things like snow peas, corn, cabbage or cauliflower.
- Substitute the noodles for organic brown rice or quinoa.
- Garnish with about a tablespoon of shredded nori.
- Finish with a tablespoon of grated daikon on top of each serving.
- Add a few drops of sesame oil to the garnish.
- Finish with a splash of umeboshi vinegar.

4 PIECES MOUNTAIN BREAD

1 AVOCADO, SLICED OR MASHED

1½ CUPS SMOKED TROUT OR SMOKED SALMON

2 CUPS ROCKET, ENGLISH SPINACH, RADICCHIO OR MIXED LEAVES

2 SPRING ONIONS, FINELY SLICED

1 CUP MINT LEAVES, TORN BASIL OR PARSLEY, ROUGHLY CHOPPED

1 SMALL CUCUMBER, SKIN ON, SLICED INTO HALF MOONS

1 CUP RED CABBAGE, SHREDDED

Mountain bread wraps [df]

Mountain bread is readily available in supermarkets. It comes in a variety of grains, but all contain some wheat. As it's such a thin bread, it's fairly easy to digest. Try to avoid the ones that are a hundred per cent wheat—instead opt for rye, millet, corn or rice. The fillings are up to you but keep to a nutritious, light and tasty balance. If you're making these wraps in cooler weather, they're great toasted too.

SERVES 4

Scrape the avocado on each piece of bread, and then top with the other ingredients. Either roll up and eat as is, or roll up and put in a flat sandwich press to toast or brown in a non-stick pan in the cooler months.

Variations

- Add a little crumbled marinated goat's feta to your wrap.
- Substitute green cabbage for the red.
- Slice fresh mushrooms—a good source of B vitamins, fibre and protein—and add into your wrap.
- Instead of smoked salmon or trout try adding sliced marinated tofu (available from supermarkets) or Yummy Tofu (*see page 154*).
- Bocconcini or buffalo mozzarella is a fabulous addition, especially when toasted first.
- Add a teaspoon of Tahini Dressing (*see page 149*) to each wrap.
- Use other spreads like hummus, pesto, soy mayonnaise, mustard, tapenade or shiro miso paste, instead of or as well as the avocado or Tahini Dressing.

Dinner

---

500 G (1 lb 1 oz) REDFISH

8 GREEN PRAWNS, SHELLED, DE-VEINED AND CHOPPED

8 CALAMARI TUBES

BIG HANDFUL EACH MINT, CORIANDER AND PARSLEY

2 GARLIC CLOVES

1 TBSP LIME JUICE

1 TSP LIME ZEST

SEA SALT AND PEPPER

2 TBSP OLIVE OIL, FOR FRYING

Stuffed calamari [df, gf]

If you can't get fresh calamari tubes, then frozen ones are a good option. Try and get them on the small side, as they will be more tender than larger ones. Cleaning calamari tubes isn't hard, just messy. If black squid ink and fishy hands turns you off, buy the cleaned and/or frozen tubes.

SERVES 4

Put all ingredients except for the tubes and oil in a food processor and blend. Check the seasoning. Stuff tubes with mixture then either chargrill, barbecue or bake until tender. The first two methods will take about three minutes on each side and baking will take about 20 minutes at 180°C (350°F). Serve with a green salad.

Variations

- Add a teaspoon of fish sauce to the stuffing for a saltier finish.
- If you bake the tubes, you can lay them on top of a can of chopped tomatoes in the baking dish. To serve, sprinkle with roughly chopped parsley and lemon wedges.
- Try adding a teaspoon or two of green curry paste and half a cup diced green beans to the ingredients in the processor.
- For fish cakes, omit the tubes. Simply add two eggs to the stuffing mixture and roll into balls then flatten. Fry in a little olive oil.

1 TBSP OLIVE OIL

1 ONION, FINELY SLICED

2 GARLIC CLOVES, CRUSHED

1 TBSP GINGER, GRATED OR SLICED

2 CARROTS, JULIENNED

2 STICKS CELERY, JULIENNED

2 RED CAPSICUM, DESEEDED AND SLICED

8 FRESH SHIITAKE MUSHROOMS

1 HEAD BROCCOLI, CUT INTO FLORETS AND STEM JULIENNED

1 CUP SNOW PEAS TAILED, STRING OFF

2 CUPS CHINESE CABBAGE, SHREDDED

2 TBSP TAMARI

1 TBSP FISH SAUCE

2 TSP SESAME OIL

1 BUNCH BOK CHOY, WASHED AND TRIMMED

1 CUP CORIANDER LEAVES, ROUGHLY CHOPPED

4 SPRING ONIONS, SLICED ON THE DIAGONAL

Basic vegetable stir-fry [*df, gf*]

Use any vegetables you like, but I think the ones I've chosen lend themselves perfectly to a stir-fry. It is okay to use frozen vegetables if they are the only thing available to make this dish, but fresh is best. Wholesome and fresh foods are a good habit to get into. Serve this stir-fry with organic brown rice, quinoa, or quinoa noodles.

SERVES 4

Heat the oil in a wok or skillet. Over a high heat stir-fry the onion, garlic and ginger for about a minute. Now, toss in all of the vegies and stir-fry with a little water (or stock if you prefer) for another minute or so. Don't overcook—keep them crunchy. Add the sauces and sesame oil with a little more water if needed—just enough so there is some liquid to use as a sauce. Turn off the heat then add the bok choy and cover with a lid for a minute to let the greens wilt. Serve garnished with coriander leaves and spring onions.

Variations

- Add organic chicken pieces with the onions if you would like a bit of meat.
- Cubed firm tofu makes for a more substantial dish. Add it with the vegies.
- Two sachets of dashi powder added with the sauces will add extra flavour.
- Add sixteen cleaned, green prawns with the onions, and cook until just pink, then remove, adding again to warm through just before serving.
- Add two tablespoons finely chopped coriander stems at the start with the garlic and ginger.
- Use any vegetables you like—baby corn, chopped green beans, cauliflower florets—when you add the other vegies.

24 GREEN PRAWNS

6 GARLIC CLOVES

2 ANCHOVIES

2 SMALL RED CHILLIES (OR TO TASTE), CHOPPED

2–4 TBSP OLIVE OIL

1 CUP ITALIAN PARSLEY, ROUGHLY CHOPPED

BIG HANDFUL BABY SPINACH

CRACKED PEPPER

SEA SALT

1 LEMON, CUT INTO WEDGES

Chilli garlic prawns [*df, gf*]

Anchovies and prawns are full of omega 3, the fish oil that is wonderful for heart health and skin. Not everyone likes the taste of anchovies but if you use them as suggested below, no-one will even know that they're in there—they'll simply add a whole lot to the flavour and goodness. The prawns are great served with crunchy spelt sourdough and a simple, green salad.

SERVES 4

Prepare the prawns by taking off the heads and shells, leaving tails intact. Clean the digestive tracts, and then wash quickly. Next, make a paste by pounding or chopping together the garlic, anchovies, chillies and 1 tablespoon of the olive oil. Rub the paste all over the prawns.

Add the rest of the oil to a hot wok and toss in the prawns. Cook for about a minute until they turn pink and lose their translucence. Turn off the heat then stir through the parsley and spinach. Season—you may or may not want to add some sea salt, but do add the cracked pepper. Serve with lemon wedges.

Variations

- When the prawns are cooked, toss them through quinoa noodles for a lovely pasta, or serve them with brown rice or quinoa grains.
- Add two tablespoons of panch phoron (Indian spice mix) in the beginning with the garlic, omitting the anchovies.

1 QUANTITY SALSA VERDE (*see page 46*)

4 SALMON FILLETS, SKIN ON

1 CAN CHICKPEAS, OR PREPARE YOUR OWN USING DRIED CHICKPEAS

½ RED ONION, SLICED

2 TOMATOES, CUT INTO WEDGES

1 AVOCADO, SLICED

HANDFUL BABY BASIL LEAVES

1 TBSP OLIVE OIL

1 TSP SEA SALT AND WHITE PEPPER

1 TBSP LEMON JUICE

1 TSP LEMON ZEST

2 CUPS COOKED BARLEY

½ CUP ITALIAN PARSLEY, ROUGHLY CHOPPED

1 TBSP OLIVE OIL

SEA SALT AND WHITE PEPPER

1 LEMON OR LIME, WEDGED, TO GARNISH

ITALIAN PARSLEY, TO GARNISH

Herbed salmon *with* barley *and* chickpea salsa [*df*]

The Salsa Verde is a beautiful accompaniment to this dish and almost any dish, in fact. It translates to 'green sauce' and is good for the liver. It's also high in folate, calcium and magnesium and it's a great way to get your greens. Use it on wraps and crackers, on top of steamed vegetables or to marinate fish, chicken, meat or tofu.

SERVES 4

Rub the salsa verde all over the salmon and leave in the fridge marinating while you prepare the rest of the dish.

Gently pound the chickpeas in a mortar and pestle or in a bowl using a fork. Don't mash until they lose their shape—keep them fairly chunky. Toss with the onion, tomatoes, avocado, basil leaves, olive oil, seasoning, lemon juice and zest. In a separate bowl, mix the barley, parsley and oil, and taste for seasoning.

To assemble, cook the salmon skin-side down for one minute or until the skin is golden brown. Using a spatula, turn fish over and cook for another minute. Divide the barley mix between four plates and then top each with a piece of salmon. Put a generous scoop of the chickpea salsa on top, letting it spill over the fish. Garnish with lemon or lime wedges and parsley.

Variation

- Add a tablespoon of finely chopped gherkins and/or green olives to the salsa verde for a different flavour.

SEA SALT AND CRACKED PEPPER
½ CUP SPELT FLOUR
4 FISH FILLETS

1–2 TBSP OLIVE OIL
1 LEMON, CUT INTO WEDGES
PARSLEY, CHOPPED, TO GARNISH

Pan-fried fish [df]

Many people don't feel confident cooking fish, which is a shame because we really should eat it at least three times a week. Once you know how to cook it properly it will encourage you to include more fish in your diet. Any fish will taste good cooked this way. Spelt is an old variety of wheat originating in Persia. It does contain gluten but is easily digested, and it's high in protein and immune-boosting properties.

SERVES 4

Season the flour well then gently press the fish into it. Shake off any excess flour and set aside. Add the oil to a hot pan and let it heat, but not smoke. Place the fish in the pan skin-side down and let cook for about two to three minutes, depending on the thickness of the fillets—until it is a nice, golden colour. Flip once only, season and cook for another two minutes. You can tell if it's cooked by sliding the tip of a sharp knife through the thickest part. If it slides in easily it's done.

Serve with lemon wedges and parsley. Don't squeeze the lemon juice over the fish until ready to eat as it will make the fish go soggy.

Variations

- Add any mix to the flour for a different flavour—try ground cumin and/or turmeric or garam masala.
- Rub in some pesto rather than flour, then cook.
- Mix chopped parsley in with the flour.
- Cut the fish into bite-sized pieces before dusting with flour—kids of all ages will like it this way.
- Coat the fish first with beaten egg, then flour, then some more egg for a thicker crust.
- For a gluten-free version use rice, LSA, buckwheat or besan (chickpea) flour.

1 LEMON
1 LARGE FILLET KINGFISH, ABOUT 500 G

SEA SALT AND WHITE OR BLACK
CRACKED PEPPER
ITALIAN PARSLEY, ROUGHLY CHOPPED

Baked kingfish *with* lemon [df, gf]

This really basic recipe is wonderful way to cook fish. As the fish keeps its juices while cooking, it comes out deliciously moist. The fish will keep cooking in the paper after it's removed from the oven or steamer, so take it off the heat just before it's cooked. Serve with Nori Chips (see page 207)

SERVES 2 TO 4

Slice the lemon into half-moon shapes, and lay half of these on a large piece of wax paper. Place the fish on top and lay the rest of the lemons on top of the fish. Scatter over some parsley and seal the paper by either folding and tucking or tying with string.

Place on an oven tray and bake for about 15 minutes at 180°C (350°F), or place in a bamboo steamer lined with wax paper, over simmering water, and steam for 10 minutes.

Variations

- Add some ginger and/or garlic into the parcel.
- Sprinkle with a teaspoon of sesame oil and add a spring onion.
- Rub the whole fish with curry paste, then add the lemon.
- Keep the lemon on the bottom and top with diced tomato, basil and garlic.

Chermoula

½ SPANISH ONION

4 CLOVES GARLIC

1 BUNCH EACH CORIANDER AND
PARSLEY, CHOPPED

1 CUP OLIVE OIL

1 TBSP CUMIN POWDER

1 TBSP TURMERIC

1 TBSP SWEET PAPRIKA

2 TSP GROUND GINGER

¾ CUP LEMON JUICE, OR TO TASTE

4 THICK WHITE FISH FILLETS LIKE
BARRAMUNDI, SNAPPER OR
BLUE-EYE TREVALLA

SEA SALT AND PEPPER, TO TASTE

½ JAP PUMPKIN, SKIN ON AND CUT
INTO THIN WEDGES

1 TSP OLIVE OIL

1 CAN CANNELLINI BEANS OR
CHICKPEAS

1 TBSP PRESERVED LEMON,
FINELY SLICED

1 CUP CORIANDER LEAVES

2 CUPS MIXED SALAD LEAVES

2 TBSP OLIVE OIL

½ CUP LEMON JUICE

EXTRA CORIANDER LEAVES, TO GARNISH

1 LEMON CUT INTO WEDGES, TO
GARNISH

Barbecued chermoula fish *with* pumpkin *and* white bean salad [*df, gf*]

Chermoula is a tasty African paste that you'll find very versatile. It will last in the fridge for months, so double the quantities and you'll have extra on hand. It's just as lovely with red or white meat or tofu.

SERVES 4

For chermoula, blend together onion and garlic. Add the fresh herbs and continue to blend with a little of the olive oil. Next, add the spices. Finally, add lemon juice to taste and enough of the remaining oil to make a smooth paste.

Rub the chermoula all over the fish fillets and season with salt. Set aside to marinate while you're preparing the rest of the dish.

Drizzle the pumpkin with olive oil and season then barbecue or bake in the oven. Cook for about three minutes on each side on the barbecue or ten minutes on each side in the oven at 200°C (400°F), until pumpkin is a golden colour.

Cook the fish for about three minutes on each side on the barbecue or in a cast-iron pan. Use a spatula rather than tongs to turn the fish as you don't want to lose any chermoula in the process. Let the fish rest for a minute or two when it comes off the heat.

Meanwhile, mix together the beans, preserved lemon, coriander and salad leaves. When the pumpkin is cooked, let it cool slightly then add it to the bean salad and give it all a gentle toss. Dress with the olive oil and lemon juice then season.

To assemble, place a mound of the bean salad on four large dinner plates. Place a piece of fish on top of the bean salad, then drizzle over a little olive oil. Garnish with lemon wedges and coriander leaves.

Variations

- Use organic chicken thighs or breasts or firm tofu instead of fish.
- Use a tablespoon of grated lemon zest instead of the preserved lemon.

Squeeze lemon juice on your food. It aids digestion and stimulates the liver.

3 BUNCHES ASPARAGUS, WOODY ENDS
BROKEN OFF

PINCH SEA SALT

2 FREE-RANGE EGGS, BOILED

1 TBSP CAPERS

1 TBSP EXTRA VIRGIN OLIVE OIL
(LEMON-INFUSED WOULD BE NICE)

1 LEMON, JUICE AND ZEST

SEA SALT AND CRACKED PEPPER

1 TBSP SHREDDED MINT

Asparagus, caper *and* egg salad [*df, gf, v*]

People often tell me they have an omelette for dinner as it's quick and easy. This salad might just take the omelette's place. The lemony sourness is delicious and the capers add a touch of saltiness that complements the soft egg.

SERVES 4

Put enough water in a flat pan so that it will cover the asparagus. Add a good pinch of sea salt. Bring the water to a gentle simmer then add the asparagus. Blanch until only just tender, about two minutes—you can tell it's ready when it's easy to slide a knife in. When ready, remove the asparagus and refresh under cold water. Drain any excess water then place on a serving plate.

Grate the eggs over the asparagus and top with the capers. Finish with a good slurp of olive oil, lemon juice and zest, seasoning and the mint.

Variation

- You can fry the capers in a little olive oil to make them crunchy and saltier. Drain before adding to the salad.

Paste

2 DRIED CHILLIES, ROASTED

1 TSP CORIANDER SEEDS, ROASTED

2 TSP SHRIMP PASTE, ROASTED (*optional*)

1 RED ONION, DICED

4 CLOVES GARLIC, CHOPPED

1 TSP LIME ZEST

1 STALK LEMONGRASS, GREEN PART ONLY, ROUGHLY CHOPPED

1 TSP GALANGAL, ROUGHLY CHOPPED

4 RED CHILLIES

¼ CUP MACADAMIAS

1 TBSP CORIANDER ROOTS AND STEMS

1 TSP TURMERIC POWDER

1 TBSP OLIVE OR SUNFLOWER OIL

1 LITRE FISH OR VEGETABLE STOCK

2 TBSP LAKSA PASTE (*see above*)

1 TBSP TAMARIND PASTE

4 PRAWNS, PEELED AND DEVEINED (LEAVE TAILS ON)

1 FLATHEAD FILLET, CUT INTO CHUNKS

1 CALAMARI TUBE, SLICED INTO 1-CM ROUNDS

4 SMALL BUNDLES RICE VERMICELLI, SOAKED IN HOT WATER

1 TBSP FISH SAUCE (*optional*)

VIETNAMESE MINT, TO GARNISH

BEAN SPROUTS, TO GARNISH

LIMES, QUARTERED, TO GARNISH

SPRING ONIONS CUT ON THE DIAGONAL, TO GARNISH

Assam laksa [*df, gf*]

This is a wheat- and coconut-free laksa. I love laksa but not the coconut-laden sauce containing all those saturated fats and hydrogenated oils you get in the take-away version. This recipe serves as a great reminder that what's good for you can be extra tasty.

SERVES 2

For the paste, pound all the ingredients together in a mortar and pestle or blitz in a food processor.

In a soup pot add the stock and the laksa and tamarind pastes and simmer for a few minutes. Now add the seafood and simmer for a minute or two until it is cooked. Taste for seasoning—if you like it saltier, add some fish sauce.

Drain the noodles and divide them between two bowls. Top with the seafood. Pour the hot broth over and garnish with mint, bean sprouts, lime quarters and spring onions.

Sides and dressings

1 CUP MINT LEAVES, FIRMLY PACKED

2 TSP BROWN SUGAR OR COCONUT PALM SUGAR

1 TSP GARAM MASALA

½ CUP LIME JUICE

1 TSP GINGER, GRATED

1 GREEN CHILLI, DE-SEEDED AND CHOPPED

6 SPRING ONIONS, CHOPPED

1 CLOVE GARLIC, CRUSHED

2 TBSP WATER

SEA SALT, TO TASTE

Fresh mint chutney [df, gf, vg, v]

This chutney gives a big hit of freshness, perfect for springtime. It is beautiful served with fish, or with rye crackers and smoked trout. Organic chicken or lamb would also taste wonderful served with a dollop of this chutney. And you might try stirring it through a curry or casserole.

MAKES ABOUT 1 CUP

Blend all the ingredients until it forms a smooth puree.

Variations

- To make coriander chutney, simply substitute fresh chopped coriander for the mint.
- Add half a cup of raw cashews.

1 CUP UNSWEETENED PEAR JUICE

1 TBSP APPLE CIDER VINEGAR

½ CUP CORIANDER LEAVES

PINCH CAYENNE PEPPER

Coriander dressing [df, gf, vg, v]

MAKES ¼ CUP

Place all ingredients in a blender and blitz until smooth.

1 BUNCH DUTCH CARROTS

2 TBSP HONEY, AGAVE, MAPLE OR
RICE SYRUP

½ CUP WATER

1 TBSP ARAME

Spring carrots [df, gf, vg, v]

Now is the time for complex sweeteners such as rice syrup, agave, honey and maple syrup. Agave syrup, made from the agave plant, is the one you might be least familiar with. After you've used any of these sweeteners, you'll understand how much better they taste than processed sugar. They are a great way to dress up your carrots.

SERVES 4

If the carrots are small, leave them whole, otherwise cut on the diagonal into one-centimetre pieces. Place in a saucepan with water, syrup and arame. Let the carrots steam until they are just tender. Remove and place on a serving plate. Let the liquid continue to simmer for another minute to reduce then pour over the carrots.

This is one season when sweeteners are recommended. That doesn't mean nasty, refined white sugar or artificial sweeteners—there's never a season or time for those. When you experience the pure pleasure of real sweetness, there's no going back to the nasty stuff. By eating these foods, and chewing them properly, your tongue actually detects the sweet taste. Try rice syrup, which is merely brown rice pounded up, then you'll realise why these types of carbohydrates are considered to be sweet. Have you ever considered how sweet fresh beetroot is? Or sweet potato? You won't crave sugar if you eat these good sugars, as your diet will be more balanced.

½ RED ONION, SLICED

3 SPRING ONIONS, FINELY CHOPPED

1 TBSP CAPERS, FINELY CHOPPED

1–2 ANCHOVIES (*optional*)

1–2 GARLIC CLOVES, CHOPPED

1 LARGE CUCUMBER, SKIN ON AND DICED

1 CUP MIXED CHOPPED HERBS, LIKE PARSLEY, MINT, CORIANDER AND BASIL

1 TOMATO, DICED (*optional*)

½ TBSP VINEGAR, LIKE TARRAGON, WHITE WINE, BROWN RICE, BALSAMIC OR UMEBOSHI

1 TBSP EXTRA VIRGIN OLIVE OIL

CRACKED BLACK OR WHITE PEPPER

1 AVOCADO, DICED

½ CUP GOAT'S FETA, DICED (*optional*)

Spring salsa [*gf*]

This is divine dolloped on top of grilled ocean trout or as a dip. A regular in my fridge.

MAKES ABOUT 2 CUPS

Gently mix together all the ingredients, adding the avocado and feta last so they don't get too mashed. Taste and adjust seasoning as necessary.

½ CUP BASIL, ROUGHLY CHOPPED

½ CUP PARSLEY, ROUGHLY CHOPPED

½ TSP THYME LEAVES (¼ TSP, IF USING DRIED)

2 SHALLOTS, ROUGHLY CHOPPED

2 TSP UMEBOSHI VINEGAR

2 TBSP APPLE JUICE CONCENTRATE OR RAW HONEY

1 TSP SEEDED MUSTARD

1 TSP WHITE PEPPER

SPLASH OF WATER

Green dressing [*df, gf, vg, v*]

MAKES ¼ CUP

Place all ingredients in a blender and blitz until smooth.

1 BUNCH EACH MINT, CORIANDER, BASIL
AND ITALIAN PARSLEY
4 SPRING ONIONS, FINELY CHOPPED
1 CLOVE GARLIC, CRUSHED

1 TBSP CAPERS, CHOPPED
1 ANCHOVY, CHOPPED
2 TBSP WHITE WINE VINEGAR
SEA SALT

Salsa verde [df, gf]

Try this combination of herbs rubbed onto a piece of organic chicken, lamb, tofu or fish then grilled. It's great for your liver and tastes as fresh as the season. Stir it through stir-fries or curries or use it as a spread on sandwiches and wraps. It's a great way to include herbs in your diet.

MAKES ABOUT 2 CUPS

Wash and dry herbs well, then chop finely and place in a large bowl with the spring onions. Make a paste by chopping together the garlic, capers and anchovy (if using). Stir this through the herbs then add the vinegar and salt. Mix to combine. Adjust seasoning as necessary.

Variations

- Add two tablespoons of fresh thyme leaves to the herb mix.
- Chevril is an interesting addition. Add ½ cup to the other herbs and chop.
- Fresh sage leaves will change the flavour completely and will go nicely with chicken, duck or red meat.

1 TBSP RED WINE VINEGAR
1 TSP POMEGRANATE MOLASSES
3 TBSP OLIVE OR SUNFLOWER OIL
1 PINK SHALLOT, FINELY DICED

1 GARLIC CLOVE, CRUSHED
1 TBSP FRESH THYME LEAVES
PINCH SEA SALT

Pomegranate dressing [df, gf, vg, v]
MAKES ¼ CUP

In a small bowl whisk together the vinegar and molasses until combined, then whisk in the oil. Add the rest of the ingredients. Put in a jar and shake. The flavours will improve after a few days when they get to know each other.

1 SMALL PURPLE CABBAGE

1 TSP SESAME OIL

1 TBSP OLIVE OR SAFFLOWER OIL

1 TSP BALSAMIC OR UMEBOSHI VINEGAR

1 TSP SEA SALT

1 TBSP TOASTED SESAME SEEDS

Purple cabbage salad [df, gf, vg, v]

There is usually a bowl of this salad in my fridge all the time. It's so good for your digestion to eat raw cabbage in spring and this salad gets better after a few days as it pickles. I add it to Mountain Bread Wraps or pan-fried fish with Tahini Dressing (see page 149), and it's simply great wilted in a pan and served with baked fish. Umeboshi vinegar is made from the umeboshi plum, a salted pickled plum that reduces acid in the body. It's also available as a paste.

SERVES 4 AS A SIDE

Shave the cabbage as finely as you can—a mandolin makes this job much easier and the end result is prettier than using a knife. Combine all the ingredients in a salad bowl (leaving out the salt if using the umeboshi vinegar), cover and refrigerate. It's great to eat straight away or leave it for a few hours so the cabbage starts to marinate in the vinegar.

Variations

- In the cooler months, sauté the salad in a little olive oil and serve as a side with a roast dinner.
- You could add a teaspoon each of chopped garlic and ginger when sautéing.
- Substitute Tamari Seeds (*see page 146*) for toasted sesame seeds and salt.
- Add a cup of grated carrot and/or baby spinach with the cabbage.
- Omit the olive oil for a lighter salad.

2 TBSP WHITE WINE VINEGAR

1 HEAPED TSP DIJON MUSTARD

1 ORANGE, JUICED

SEA SALT AND PEPPER

Basic oil-free dressing [df, gf, vg, v]

MAKES ABOUT 1½ CUPS

Place all the ingredients in a jar with a lid. Shake well.

½ CUP ORANGE JUICE

1 TSP BROWN RICE VINEGAR

1 TSP UMEBOSHI VINEGAR

1 TBSP RICE SYRUP OR HONEY

1 TBSP CORIANDER AND MINT LEAVES, CHOPPED

Oil-free dressing [df, gf, vg, v]
MAKES ABOUT ¾ CUP

Place all the ingredients in a jar with a lid. Shake well.

1 TBSP FLAX OIL

1 TBSP LIME JUICE

1 TSP TAMARI

1 GARLIC CLOVE, CRUSHED

½ TSP WASABI

Green vegetable dressing or tuna marinade [df, gf, vg, v]
MAKES ¼ CUP

Combine all ingredients then pour over green vegies or fish. You can also use this dressing as a marinade.

Variation
- Add a teaspoon of grated ginger.

Sweet things

2 CUPS SPELT FLOUR

PINCH SALT

2 CUPS SOY MILK OR
ALMOND MILK

OMEGA SPREAD OR SUNFLOWER OIL,
TO FRY

Crepes [df, vg, v]

These are so good simply drizzled with a little maple syrup and topped with fresh fruit or, in the cooler months, try them filled with a little Fruit Compote (see page 219) and top with unsweetened thick yoghurt.

MAKES ABOUT 8 CREPES

Sift the flour and salt in a bowl. Gradually pour the milk in a steady stream into the flour, whisking as you go to avoid a lumpy batter. The mixture should be the consistency of pouring cream.

Warm a non-stick pan and lightly grease. Pour about a third of a cup of the batter into the pan and swirl to spread evenly. Cook the crepe for one minute or until little bubbles appear. Flip, cooking the other side for another minute or so, until crepe is golden. Remove to a plate and cover with a clean tea towel; continue with remaining batter. Be warned, the first crepe will normally be a dud, but the rest should come out perfectly.

Variations

- Substitute one cup of buckwheat for one cup of spelt flour for a nuttier flavour.
- For a gluten-free crepe use besan (chickpea) flour instead of spelt.

Spelt is wheat and contains gluten, but is easy for most of us to digest. On top of that it is high in protein and a good immunity booster.

¼ CUP SAGO

1 CUP WATER

¾–1 CUP ALMOND OR COCONUT MILK

⅓ CUP SWEETENER, LIKE GRATED
COCONUT PALM SUGAR, AGAVE OR
MAPLE SYRUP (*optional*)

2 TBSP DESICCATED OR SHREDDED
COCONUT (*optional*)

Topping

THREE FRUITS; FOR EXAMPLE THE
FLESH FROM TWO MANGO CHEEKS,
A CUP OF ANY BERRIES, OR ½ CUP
PASSIONFRUIT PULP

1 CUP SUGAR-FREE FRUIT JUICE, LIKE
PEAR, APPLE, STRAWBERRY

3 TSP AGAR AGAR FLAKES

Sago fruit cups [*df, gf, vg, v*]

Sago has a lovely texture and lends itself well to desserts. You can leave out the agar agar and simply serve this in a bowl with fruit and a sweetener.

MAKES 4 DESSERT CUPS

In a non-stick pot, cook the sago in the water until soft. This will take around 30 minutes. Drain and place in a bowl, then stir through the milk. Now stir in the sweetener (if using) and allow the mixture to cool.

Spoon the sago into glasses, filling halfway. Top with a layer of coconut (if using) and put the glasses on a tray in the fridge to allow them to cool slightly while you prepare the fruit topping.

Prepare one fruit at a time. Place it in a processor and blend with enough juice to make a puree. Sieve to remove any air bubbles then put this mixture into a shallow pan with a teaspoon of agar agar. Bring to a simmer, then simmer until the agar agar dissolves and thickens, about ten minutes. Let the mixture cool slightly.

Top the sago cups with the fruit puree and put the cups back in the fridge to cool and set before serving.

Variations

- Add a tablespoon of granola or toasted muesli between the layers for a bit of crunch.
- Drizzle a teaspoon of hulled tahini between the layers, with or without the granola.

Base

1 CUP RICE FLOUR

1 CUP ALMONDS OR HAZELNUTS

2 TSP GROUND CINNAMON

1 TSP GROUND GINGER

1 TBSP AGAVE OR MAPLE SYRUP

⅓ CUP SUNFLOWER OIL OR OMEGA SPREAD

1 TSP VANILLA ESSENCE

PINCH OF SALT

Filling

450 G (16 oz) DAIRY-FREE DARK CHOCOLATE

180 G (6 oz) TUB SILKEN TOFU

1 SHOT ESPRESSO OR 30 ML STRONG INSTANT COFFEE

1 TSP VANILLA ESSENCE

⅓ CUP COCONUT PALM SUGAR, GRATED OR RAW SUGAR (*optional*)

Vegan chocolate cheesecake
[*df, gf, vg, v*]

This is a seriouly rich chocolate dessert and one that will surprise anyone who doubts that vegan food can taste this good. You can also use almost any filling you like with this yummy base.

SERVES 8

Heat oven to 160°C (315°F) and lightly grease a 24-centimetre spring-form pie tin with Omega spread or sunflower oil.

For the base, put the dry ingredients in a food processor and blitz until the mixture resembles fine breadcrumbs. Add the syrup, oil, vanilla essence and salt and blitz until the mixture comes together into a ball. Press the mixture into the base and up the sides of the pie tin. Bake for 15 minutes then set aside.

For the filling, melt the chocolate in a bowl over a simmering pot of water then allow to cool slightly. Process the tofu until smooth then stir it through the chocolate—the mixture should stiffen up now. Then, stir in the coffee, vanilla and sweetener (if using).

Pour the filling into the pie dish and bake at 160°C (315°F) for 20 minutes. Allow to cool before taking it out of the tin.

Variation

- Serve with loads of berries piled on top.

Drinks

1 BUNCH MINT
4 TBSP BLACK TEA
4 TBSP EVAPORATED CANE SUGAR,
RAW HONEY, DEMURA SUGAR OR AGAVE

1½ LITRES BOILING WATER
PINE NUTS, FOR GARNISH

Moroccan mint tea [*df, gf, vg, v*]

Mint is a very cooling herb and is perfect to have in spring. A complex sugar is also recommended at this time of year, so this tea is lovely. It's a great digestive after a big meal or on a hot afternoon. I often chill it and serve in beautiful tall glasses.

SERVES 4

In a large teapot add the mint, black tea and your choice of sweetener. Pour over the water and let the ingredients infuse for a few minutes. Strain into cups and garnish with pine nuts.

2 FROZEN BANANAS, CHOPPED
3 CUPS COLD SOY, RICE OR ALMOND MILK

2 SHOTS ESPRESSO, COOLED
GROUND CINNAMON, TO GARNISH

Morning-after smoothie [*df, gf, vg, v*]

Bananas are perfect for smoothies and particularly the 'morning after'. It is recommended though that you eat them in moderation only, as in Chinese medicine they are considered to cause phlegm and are energetically cold.

SERVES 2

Place the chopped bananas and a little milk in a blender and whizz to a smooth consistency. Add the rest of the milk a little at a time, blending after each addition, then add the coffee. Pour into two tall glasses and sprinkle with cinnamon. Crazy!

1 POMEGRANATE
120 ML (4 fl oz) CAMPARI

400 ML (13 fl oz) BLOOD ORANGE JUICE
(SPARKLING OR STILL)
ICE (*optional*)

Pomegranate, Campari *and* organic blood orange [*df, gf, vg, v*]

Pomegranates are one of those fruits with a long history of health-giving features. They're considered to have aphrodisiac and anti-cancer properties, to aid fertility, to increase iron levels and are full of betacarotene. I recommend you try them, and the seeds are also lovely over salads. And Campari is a wonderful aperitif and is a great drink to have before meals.
SERVES 4

Cut the pomegranate in half and remove the lovely red seeds using your fingers. Avoid the white piths. Put the Campari, blood orange juice and pomegranate seeds in the blender. Blend with some ice until smooth, then strain.

Variations

- Pomegranates are a winter fruit, so feel free to substitute summer fruits in the warmer months.
- Adding a good splash of mineral water rather than juice is nice, or try half and half.
- Add a few mint leaves to the blender for a hint of freshness.
- Add 120 ml of vodka to the mix.

Try to avoid wearing black now as it's the season to be jolly. Wear colours. Eat colourful food too.

Summer

Spring may be over, but temperatures naturally vary from region to region so you may want to still *eat mostly cooked foods* in early summer. When the temperature starts to creep up you should introduce more *raw foods* into your diet, so that at the height of summer you will be eating lots of raw foods with your meals.

Late summer is considered the fifth season in Traditional Chinese Medicine. It's when summer and autumn come together and you'll be drawn outside, encouraged to enjoy your life. Food at this time is not such a priority, so you will tend to *eat more lightly* than any other time of the year. It's important not to burden your body with anything heavy right now, emotionally or physically.

Object

The object is to let your energy flow 'out'. You'll want to expel from your body the last of the stored heat of winter. To aid this, induce sweat by eating spicy food. It's time to get outside and enjoy the sun, sea and other people.

Organ

The organs most sensitive in the earlier part of summer are the heart and small intestine. In late summer it's the spleen and stomach.

Emotion

The emotions stored in your heart and small intestine are joy, happiness and playfulness. The emotions associated with an overworked spleen/stomach are worry and obsessive thoughts.

Symptoms

The heart and small intestine rule the tongue, blood vessels and your complexion. The spleen and stomach look after the mouth, muscles and lips. So in early summer you may experience an irregular heartbeat, wild dreams, a scattered mind, confused thoughts, speech problems, depression, insomnia, poor memory and circulation, or a very red or pale face. You may also experience physical conditions like weight gain, poor digestion, flabbiness, fatigue, nausea, abdominal bloating, blood-sugar imbalance and loose stools, in varying degrees.

Flavour & foods

- The flavour associated with the heart/small intestine is bitter—bitter foods, such as lettuce, watercress, endive, turnip, celery, asparagus, alfalfa, rye, oats, quinoa and amaranth are said to put joy in our hearts.

- Later in summer it is recommended that you add sweet flavours from complex carbohydrates and sweeteners—rice, maple and agave syrups, and honey—to your diet.
- The foods to eat in summer are more raw foods, salads, legumes and juices; as well as sprouts, especially mung and soy beans and alfalfa; fruit like apples, watermelon, limes and lemon; cucumber; tofu; and hot spices such as fresh ginger.
- Horseradish and black pepper are great to help to induce sweat.
- Use culinary herbs like chrysanthemum, mint and chamomile in your cooking and tea at this time of year.

Cooking methods

As simple, light food is recommended, you'll be able to reduce the amount of time spent cooking. Cook over a high heat using less water, oil and salt. Make food preparation quick and easy so you can get outside to revel in the joy and abundance that summer brings.

Avoid

In early summer stay away from cold substances like iced drinks and ice cream, as these foods are contracting—they hold in sweat, toxins and heat. Also avoid heavy foods such as meat, grains, seeds, dairy, oil and eggs. Eaten in excess, these will make you sluggish during summer.

In late summer avoid refined sugar and carbohydrates, too much alcohol, complex food combinations, large meals, a sedentary lifestyle and eating your evening meal after 8 pm. Remember to keep hydrated during these months by drinking lots of clean, room-temperature water.

Fresh in summer

Fruit: apricot / banana / berry / cherry / lychee / mango / melon / orange / passionfruit / pineapple / avocado / tomato / watercress / zucchini / peach / nectarine / plum / squash / fig / apple / grape / kiwifruit / lemon / pear / rhubarb / gooseberry / elderflower / currant

Vegetables: lettuce / asparagus / green bean / borlotti bean / snake bean / butter bean / capsicum / celery / cucumber / eggplant / spring onion / green pea / snow pea / sugar snap pea / radish / sweetcorn / daikon / leek / caper

Seafood: Atlantic salmon / Australian salmon / tiger flathead / gold band snapper / tuna / abalone / blue swimmer crab / Sydney rock oyster / bay prawn / school prawn / rock lobster / anchovy / yabby / marron

Breakfast

500 G (18 oz) FRESH RICOTTA

2 LARGE FREE-RANGE EGGS

2 TBSP INTERESTING HONEY, LIKE ONE
WITH A CITRUS FLAVOUR

½ TBSP GROUND CINNAMON

4 SLICES RYE SOURDOUGH BREAD

4 MANGO CHEEKS, SLICED

Baked sweet ricotta *with* mango cheeks [*gf, v*]

This is one of the few times I've used dairy and bread in this book. White cheese is not as fatty as yellow cheese so a little occasionally is fine. This makes a really lovely Sunday breakfast and if there are any leftovers, it will keep through the week.

SERVES 4

Preheat your oven to 150°C (300°F). Mix together the ricotta, eggs, honey and cinnamon. Put the mixture into a lined, non-stick loaf tin (25 x 10 cm), cover with foil and place inside a larger roasting pan. Fill the roasting pan with enough warm water to reach halfway up the side of the loaf tin. Bake for 45 to 60 minutes until the ricotta is firm. Allow to cool completely before turning out.

Chargrill or toast the bread. Slice the ricotta and serve with mango cheeks and bread.

Variation

- You could drizzle some extra honey over the top and sprinkle with cinnamon. Yum!

½ CUP ALMONDS, FINELY CHOPPED

½ CUP OATMEAL (GROUND OATS, NOT FLAKES)

1 LIME OR LEMON, JUICE AND ZEST

2 TBSP MAPLE SYRUP, AGAVE SYRUP, RAW HONEY OR RICE SYRUP

2 CUPS NATURAL YOGHURT

Oat *and* almond yoghurt [v]

Yoghurt is a light and nutritious breakfast. Adding complex carbohydrates like oats and almonds will keep you feeling full for longer so you won't have those cravings for snacks between meals. Be sure to chew this dish well to benefit from its goodness.

SERVES 2

Mix together the almonds and oats and spread evenly on a baking tray. Place under a hot grill for about two minutes. Stir a few times to make sure the mix browns evenly and doesn't burn. Allow to cool.

Combine the zest and juice with your choice of sweetener then stir it into the yoghurt. Fold the yoghurt through the almond mixture.

Spoon the mixture into two glasses and chill before serving.

Variations

- Use other grain or nut meals instead of oats—try almond meal, ground spelt or millet meal.
- To make this breakfast look even prettier and healthier, add goji berries, which are the richest source of carotenoids of all known foods and have 500 times the vitamin C of oranges.
- To complete the dish, you might sprinkle the top with LSA before serving.

Eat good, complex sugars to prevent craving those naughty, refined sugars. Try sweeteners like agave, rice or maple syrup and raw honey.

3 CUPS WATERMELON
½ CUP PLAIN GOAT'S YOGHURT

2 TSP GINGER, GRATED
2 LIMES, JUICE AND ZEST

Watermelon frappé [gf, v]

Watermelon is recommended in summer as it's so cooling. Goat's yoghurt is high in protein and is anti-inflammatory, so it may help deal with any allergies at this time of year. You'll love the zing of the ginger and limes in this gloriously pink frappé.

SERVES 2

Place all ingredients in a blender and blitz until smooth. Serve in two tall glasses.

2 MANGOES
2 TBSP LSA

2 TSP AGAVE SYRUP

Mango, LSA *and* agave syrup
[df, gf, vg, v]

LSA is the common abbreviation for a mixture of crushed linseeds, sunflower seeds and almonds. It's a great way to start the day as it's full of fibre and protein, will keep you feeling full longer and tastes great. Linseeds (or flaxseeds) are also good to help balance your hormones. The nutty flavour of the LSA with the sweetness of the fruit in this recipe is delicious.

SERVES 4

Slice the cheeks off the mangoes, cut the flesh into cubes and scoop out of the skin. Divide the cubes between two plates and sprinkle with the LSA and syrup.

Lunch

---

2 CUPS FRESH BROAD BEANS

2 CUPS FREEKAH, COOKED

1 SMALL RED ONION, FINELY SLICED

1 GARLIC CLOVE, CRUSHED

2 TOMATOES, DICED

1 LEBANESE CUCUMBER, DICED

1 CUP EACH MINT AND PARSLEY LEAVES,
ROUGHLY CHOPPED

3 TBSP EXTRA VIRGIN OLIVE OIL

1 LEMON, ZEST ONLY

1 TSP UMEBOSHI VINEGAR OR
LEMON JUICE

2 TSP SEA SALT

Broad bean *and* freekah salad
[df, vg, v]

Freekah is a type of wheat grain that is picked young and then smoked over barley. It is packed with nutrients and is very easy to digest, unlike our modern wheat grain. It has a chewy texture and a nutty flavour and is available either whole or cracked.

SERVES 2

To cook the broad beans, steam them in a little water for about one minute, until just tender. Drain, then cool them enough to handle. Then take off their inner skins.

In a large bowl, toss together all of the ingredients. Taste for seasoning and adjust if necessary.

2 CANS CANNELLINI BEANS, DRAINED
AND RINSED, OR PREPARE YOUR OWN
USING DRIED BEANS AND KOMBU

½ RED ONION, DICED OR SLICED

1 LEBANESE CUCUMBER, SKIN LEFT ON
AND DICED

1 CUP MIXED HERBS LIKE BASIL, MINT
AND PARSLEY, ROUGHLY CHOPPED

1 TBSP LEMON ZEST

1–2 TBSP EACH OLIVE OIL AND
LEMON JUICE

SEA SALT AND GROUND WHITE PEPPER

Basic bean salad [*df, gf, vg, v*]

Legumes are a great source of plant protein and fibre as well as being one of the best anti-ageing foods. This is a good basic salad recipe but the possibilities for dishes using these 'wonder foods' are endless. See the variations below, then it's over to you for your favourite ways of reinventing my basic bean salad!

SERVES 4

Place the beans, onion, cucumbers, herbs and zest in a large bowl and mix to combine. Drizzle with the oil and lemon juice and season. Mix again.

Variations

- Mix in a cup of fresh, steamed broad beans, chopped green beans, peas, or any type of sprout.
- Add a finely chopped garlic clove or two.
- Arame adds a lovely flavour—soak one tablespoon in water or brown rice vinegar, then drain before mixing in.
- Use a third of a cup each of pepitas, sesame and sunflower seeds or half a cup of Tamari Seeds (*see page 146*) or chopped walnuts for crunch.
- Throw in a cup of smoked trout.
- Add two cups of roasted pumpkin or sweet potato.
- A cup of any leftover whole grains can be mixed in—freekah, barley or organic brown rice, or spelt, for example.
- Dice and add one avocado.
- For a little bit of pungency add one tablespoon of vinegar such as umeboshi, red wine, brown rice or a good balsamic.
- Extra colour can be achieved with two big handfuls of baby spinach or rocket and a diced tomato.
- Add a cup of diced celery.
- Finely chop two spring onions and add.
- Add other herbs like chives, coriander, thyme.

1 BUNCH EACH ITALIAN AND
CURLY PARSLEY

1 BUNCH MINT

4 SPRING ONIONS, FINELY CHOPPED

2 CLOVES GARLIC, CRUSHED

1 LEBANESE CUCUMBER, PEELED
AND DICED

1 CUP COOKED QUINOA, NICE AND DRY

1 CAN BROWN LENTILS OR
1½ CUPS COOKED BROWN LENTILS WITH
1 STICK KOMBU

2 TBSP OLIVE OIL

2 LEMONS, JUICED

SEA SALT, TO TASTE

Tabouli [df, gf, vg, v]

*This Mediterranean salad just got healthier: I've added the lentils to make it a complete
protein and used quinoa instead of cracked wheat. I find it difficult to digest burghul (cracked
wheat) and I would've been very sad to give up Tabouli because of that, so I'm thrilled by this
recipe and I think it may be even better than the original.*

SERVES 4 AS A SIDE

Fill your sink with water and let the herbs soak in it to remove
any dirt. Drain on a tea towel until dry (a salad spinner will
also do the job beautifully), then chop finely—discard the mint
stems but chop the parsley stems. Add all the herbs to a large
bowl with the spring onion, garlic, cucumber, quinoa and lentils.
Combine the oil, lemon juice and salt and dress the salad. Mix
everything together well. You might like it a bit saltier, or with
more lemon or garlic. Adjust the seasoning to your liking.

Variations

- Add two diced vine-ripened tomatoes.
- Mix in one diced capsicum.
- Use cracked freekah instead of the quinoa.

spelt with spelt
flakes (rolled spelt)

yeasted...
seedy spelt...
sourdough

organic
cornbread
sourdough

...dough
...=lindseed, barley
& sunflower)

4 FREE-RANGE EGGS

1 TSP MIRIN (*optional*)

PINCH WHITE PEPPER

3 TBSP OLIVE OIL

3 SPRING ONIONS, WHITE AND GREEN PARTS SEPARATED, SLICED

2 GARLIC CLOVES, CRUSHED

2 TSP GINGER, GRATED

2 TBSP CORIANDER STEMS, CHOPPED

1 LONG RED CHILLI, CHOPPED (*optional*)

2 ANCHOVIES (*optional*)

2 STICKS CELERY, DICED

2 CORN COBS, KERNELS REMOVED

1 CUP GREEN BEANS, FINELY SLICED

1 CARROT, DICED

1 TBSP FISH SAUCE

1–2 TSP TAMARI

1 TSP SESAME OIL

4 CUPS COOKED ORGANIC BROWN RICE (PREFERABLY COOKED THE DAY BEFORE AS IT WILL BE DRIER)

1 CUP CORIANDER, PARSLEY AND/OR MINT LEAVES, CHOPPED

Good fried rice [*df, gf*]

I think this is one of my favourite dishes. I know I'm getting all the food groups I need in one dish, it tastes so good and it's an ideal way to use up leftover rice or vegies. A perfect lunch. And this rice improves the next day once the flavours have got to know each other.

SERVES 4

Whisk eggs with the mirin and seasoning until fluffy. Using half the oil, grease the pan and pour the eggs in. Let one side of the omelette brown, then flip to cook the other side. Remove from the heat, roll up and slice. Set aside.

Heat the rest of the oil in a wok or large skillet and add the white parts of the spring onions, garlic, ginger, coriander and chilli and stir-fry for a minute. Add the anchovies now if using (they dissolve leaving a depth of flavour second-to-none). Toss in all the vegies and sauté until almost soft. Now add the sauces and sesame oil and stir. Next add the rice, stir to combine and heat through. Gently fold through the egg with the herbs and green parts of the spring onions, and adjust seasoning. Serve hot or at room temperature.

Variations

- In the macrobiotic diet principles it is recommended that you use short-grain rice in winter and long-grain in summer.
- Add a cup of cubed smoked tofu with the vegetables.
- Substitute lightly steamed peas for the green beans.

1 PKT BUCKWHEAT NOODLES

2 TBSP ARAME, SOAKED IN ½ CUP WATER UNTIL SOFT

1 CUP DAIKON, CUT INTO MATCHSTICKS

1 CARROT, CUT INTO MATCHSTICKS

1 CUP SMOKED TOFU, CUT INTO MATCHSTICKS

½ CUP TAMARI

2 TBSP WHITE WINE VINEGAR

2 TBSP MIRIN

1½ TBSP SESAME OIL

⅓ CUP SESAME SEEDS, GROUND

1 CUP BABY DAIKON SPROUTS, OR ANY OTHER SPROUTS

1 SHEET TOASTED NORI, SHREDDED

Buckwheat, smoked tofu, daikon *and* arame salad [*df, gf, vg, v*]

This delicious salad contains two kinds of sea vegetable: arame and nori. Arame is high in calcium and iodine and nori has a high-protein content and is easily digested. I love cooking with sea vegetables because they're so tasty and convenient to use. In this recipe I've included buckwheat noodles as they're gluten-free. Buckwheat can also improve circulation and strengthen digestion.

SERVES 4

Cook the noodles according to the instructions on the packet. Drain and set aside to dry out a little. Drain the arame and keep the liquid.

Put the daikon, carrot, tofu, noodles and arame in a bowl and gently mix together. For the sauce, mix the soaking liquid from the arame together with the Tamari, vinegar, mirin, sesame oil and sesame seeds. Drizzle over the noodles and top with the sprouts and nori.

Dinner

1 BUNCH CORIANDER, ROUGHLY CHOPPED
1 CHILLI, CHOPPED
2 STALKS LEMONGRASS, WHITE PART ONLY, FINELY CHOPPED
1 TBSP GINGER, GRATED
2 KAFFIR LIME LEAVES, SLICED
1 TSP SESAME OIL

1 TSP SEA SALT
1 × 2 KG (4 lb 4 oz) WHOLE BARRAMUNDI
1 LIME, SLICED
BANANA LEAVES, TO WRAP
½ CUP CORIANDER LEAVES
1 TBSP OLIVE OIL

Barramundi *in* a banana leaf, Thai style [*df, gf*]

Steaming is a healthy way to cook fish. It keeps all the juices in so none of the nutrients are lost and the fish stays moist and flavoursome. You can choose another fish if you can't find barramundi but make sure that it's a fairly fleshy fish like snapper, jewfish, salmon or tuna.

SERVES 4

Pound or blitz the coriander, chilli, lemongrass, ginger, lime leaves, sesame oil and salt into a paste. Rub the paste all over both sides of the fish. Lay half the lime slices on the banana leaf then place the fish on top. Drizzle with the olive oil. Place coriander leaves and the rest of the lime slices on top. It's also nice to stuff the fish with the coriander leaves and lime wedges if you have extra. Wrap the fish inside the banana leaves and secure with string. Depending on the size of your fish, you may use just one banana leaf or a few and overlap them.

Place the fish parcel on the barbecue, or in the oven for 15 minutes at 180°C (350°F), and cook until fish is tender; about 7 minutes on each side if barbecuing. The fish is cooked when it comes away from the bone easily when gently pulled apart with a knife. To serve, place the parcel on a platter. Open up the parcel to expose the fish and use the leaf as a base to keep the juices in while you serve the fish. Remember banana leaves are not edible.

Lemongrass paste

4 STALKS LEMONGRASS, INNER WHITE
PART ONLY

½ BUNCH EACH CORIANDER LEAVES AND
STEMS AND MINT LEAVES

2-CM PIECE GINGER

FRESH OR DRIED CHILLI TO TASTE

SEA SALT TO TASTE

4 FRESH SALMON FILLETS

BAMBOO SKEWERS, SOAKED IN WATER

Chilli lime dressing

1 TBSP WHITE PALM SUGAR, GRATED

½ CUP HOT WATER

1 FRESH RED CHILLI, FINELY CHOPPED

4 LIMES, JUICED

2 TSP FISH SAUCE

1 CARROT, GRATED

LARGE HANDFUL OF BABY SPINACH

SMALL HANDFUL CORIANDER LEAVES

Thai salmon skewers *and* salad
[*df, gf*]

Spicy foods should be eaten in the warmer months and avoided during winter. The ginger and chilli in this dish will help induce sweat, assisting your body to expel toxins. Buy beautiful fresh fish from your favourite fishmonger. You should aim to eat fish at least three times a week and these skewers make it a pleasure to cook and devour!

SERVES 4

For the paste, roughly chop all the ingredients and blitz in a food processor or blender, or pound together in a mortar and pestle. You should end up with a chunky paste.

Chop the salmon into 2-centimetre pieces. Rub the fish with the paste and thread onto the wet skewers (being wet, the skewers are less like to burn). Let the fish marinate for at least 10 minutes.

For the dressing, dilute the palm sugar in the water and then add the other ingredients. Taste and adjust the seasoning as necessary.

When ready to serve, place the carrot, baby spinach and coriander leaves in a bowl with a little dressing (reserve at least a couple of tablespoons) and toss. Place the salad in a big mound on the side of four plates. Chargrill or grill your salmon skewers for about 1 minute on each side, making sure the salmon remains pink. Gently place the skewers up against the salad and drizzle with the reserved dressing. Yum!

Mango salsa

4 MANGOES, FLESH DICED

½ CUP LIME JUICE

½ CUP CORIANDER LEAVES,
ROUGHLY CHOPPED

1 MEDIUM CHILLI, FINELY DICED

½ RED ONION, DICED

1 TSP FISH SAUCE (*optional*)

1 TBSP OLIVE OIL

1 TSP SEA SALT

1 TSP WHITE PEPPER

1 PKT MUGWORT SOBA OR OTHER
WHOLEGRAIN NOODLES

2 TBSP ARAME

ZEST OF ½ ORANGE

½ CUP ORANGE JUICE

1 TSP WHITE PEPPER

1 TSP UMEBOSHI VINEGAR (*optional*)

4 BARRAMUNDI FILLETS

CORIANDER LEAVES AND LIME WEDGES,
TO GARNISH

Barramundi *with* mango salsa *and* soba noodles [*df*]

Steaming fish is recommended in summer. A bamboo steamer is useful to have for any kind of steaming. They're available in Asian grocery shops and are inexpensive to buy. Mugwort (a herb that is high in iron) soba noodles are commonly found in Japanese cuisine and have a soft, silky texture that is lovely with the fish and salsa. But you could use any wholegrain noodle instead.

SERVES 4

Gently combine all of the salsa ingredients and set aside. Cook the noodles in plenty of water until al dente. Lay the arame on the bottom of a colander and drain the noodles over it. Let cool. In a bowl, combine the orange zest and juice, pepper and vinegar. Steam fish either in a bamboo steamer for about five minutes, or wrap in wax paper and put in the oven for ten minutes at 180°C (350°F).

Place noodles in a large bowl and gently mix with the orange juice dressing. Divide the noodles evenly between four plates, and then top with the fish. Add a generous spoonful of the salsa and garnish with coriander leaves and lime wedges.

4 TEMPEH PATTIES OR 1 BLOCK

4 TBSP TAMARI OR SHOYU

2 ONIONS, SLICED

OLIVE OIL

4 SPELT SOURDOUGH BURGER BUNS

4 TBSP SOY MAYONNAISE

1 CUP EACH BEETROOT AND CARROT, GRATED

1 AVOCADO, SLICED

2 CUPS MIXED SALAD LEAVES

Tempeh burger [*df, vg, v*]

Enjoying a burger doesn't mean you have to eat meat. This recipe is ideal for the nutty, fermented flavour of tempeh, which is high in plant-based protein and vitamin B12, and low in fat. You can buy tempeh in a block or as patties. If you're a tempeh novice, start using it like this so it is mixed with other strong flavours. Once you get a taste for it, you'll use it in other dishes, for sure.

SERVES 4

If you've bought a block of tempeh, slice it through the middle width-ways and again lengthwise. Marinate the tempeh in the soy sauce while you prepare your burger.

Barbecue or sauté the onions in olive oil. Grill, barbecue, chargrill, bake or pan-fry the tempeh until golden brown. Toast your bun—it's lovely done on a chargrill. Put some mayonnaise on the bun and top the burger with the other ingredients, as you would any burger.

4 KINGFISH FILLETS, THINLY SLICED

2 LIMES, JUICED

1 SPANISH ONION, FINELY SLICED

2 CUPS CORIANDER LEAVES,
ROUGHLY CHOPPED

2 CUPS COCONUT MILK

2 TBSP FISH SAUCE

1 SMALL RED CHILLI, DE-SEEDED
AND CHOPPED

JASMINE RICE, TO SERVE

12 ASPARAGUS SPEARS

Cured Thai kingfish [df, gf]

Raw fish is not everyone's idea of heaven, but you'll love this dish. Lime juice helps you digest the fat from coconut milk and the chillies will boost your metabolism. I always keep a bottle of fish sauce to hand as it adds piquancy to dishes and provides that quintessential Thai flavour. And the medium-chain fatty acids in the coconut are great to aid weight loss and reduce bad cholesterol.

SERVES 4

Combine the fish and lime juice in a ceramic or glass bowl. Cover and marinate in the fridge for about an hour or until the fish turns white and appears cooked. Drain the liquid and combine it with the onion, coriander, coconut milk, fish sauce and chilli. Pour the mixture over fish and marinate for at least two hours in the fridge.

Steam the rice according to the instructions on the packet. Cut the woody ends off the asparagus and blanch in salted, simmering water until just tender. Refresh in cold water to stop them cooking. Cut the spears into long quarters. Divide the fish between four plates and top with the asparagus. Drizzle with the marinade and serve with rice.

Variation

• Use snapper or scallops instead of kingfish.

Dipping sauce

1½ LITRES FILTERED WATER

2 TSP GINGER, GRATED

4 SPRING ONIONS, SLICED DIAGONALLY

3 SACHETS DASHI

1 TBSP TAMARI OR SHOYU

½ TBSP MIRIN (*optional*)

2 TBSP PALM SUGAR, GRATED

1 PKT BUCKWHEAT NOODLES

2 SPRING ONIONS, SLICED DIAGONALLY

4 TBSP DAIKON, GRATED

½ SHEET NORI, SHREDDED

Chilled buckwheat soba *with* dipping sauce *and* shredded nori [*df, gf*]

Use 100 per cent buckwheat noodles for this recipe to ensure a gluten-free dish. Buckwheat improves the appetite and strengthens digestion. It also contains rutin, a bioflavonoid that may reduce blood pressure and improve circulation to hands and feet. Dashi is a powdered stock consisting of shiitake mushrooms, kombu and bonito (fish) flakes. You can also buy vegetarian dashi if you prefer to make a vegan dish.

SERVES 4

Place all the dipping sauce ingredients in a saucepan and simmer over low heat until the sugar has dissolved. Meanwhile, cook the noodles as directed on the packet.

Divide the noodles—either warm (in cooler weather) or chilled (on hot days)—between individual, small Japanese bowls and top with spring onions, daikon and nori. Serve the sauce in separate dishes on the side or pour over the top.

4 MEDIUM BEETROOT, LEAVES CUT OFF

2 TBSP EXTRA VIRGIN OLIVE OIL

1 TBSP BALSAMIC VINEGAR

1 GARLIC CLOVE, CRUSHED (*optional*)

SEA SALT AND CRACKED PEPPER

1 BIG BUNCH WATERCRESS

1 CUP WALNUT HALVES

½ CUP SUNFLOWER SEEDS

1 CUP MARINATED FETA

HANDFUL BASIL LEAVES

Beetroot, watercress *and* goat's feta salad [*df, gf, v*]

Watercress is a wonderful herb. It aids weight loss, is high in calcium and folate, and will help clean out your liver. The roasted sunflower seeds and walnuts give texture and crunch and provide good oils in your diet. And the natural sweetness of the beetroot contrasts beautifully with the saltiness of the feta. This well-balanced salad will give you a really satisfying lunch or light dinner.

SERVES 2

Wash the beetroot and put into a deep saucepan covered with water. Simmer for 30 minutes or until tender when poked with a skewer or small knife. Let them cool, then put them under running cold water—the skin will come away easily, as will the furry bits. You will be left with lovely, plump, smooth-looking vegetables. Cut them into quarters and set aside while you prepare the salad.

Combine the oil, vinegar, garlic (if using) and seasoning in a bottle or jar and shake well.

Wash the watercress well and dry. If the watercress has lots of woody stems these will need to be removed—you may lose quite a bit of a seemingly big bunch after doing this. Place the nuts and seeds in a pan (a heavy-based cast iron skillet will serve you well, but is not essential) and dry fry the seeds over a medium heat until they start to go a lovely golden colour. Remove from the pan and let them cool slightly on a plate.

On a gorgeous big platter lay down half the watercress. Lightly dress with the oil mix and season to taste. Then top with roughly half the beetroot, walnut and seed mix, feta and basil. Finish with another layer of the watercress and other ingredients, then dress and season again.

Variations

- Use baby spinach, rocket, mixed leaves or radicchio instead of watercress.
- Feta in brine will also work well—it just won't be as creamy, which is actually better in summer, and it has less fat.
- Try raspberry, white balsamic or white wine vinegar.

Sides and dressings

1 BUNCH ROCKET, WASHED

1 FENNEL BULB, SHAVED WITH A
MANDOLIN, PEELER OR KNIFE

½ RADICCHIO, WASHED AND LEAVES
LEFT WHOLE

1 TBSP OLIVE OIL

2 TBSP LEMON OR ORANGE JUICE

1 TBSP LEMON OR ORANGE ZEST

1 CLOVE GARLIC, CRUSHED

SALT AND WHITE PEPPER

Rocket salad [df, gf, vg, v]

You might choose to use only rocket but I highly recommend adding the other ingredients at least some of the time. The fennel is wonderful for weight loss and the radicchio has a bitter flavour (recommended in summer), which helps more effective digestion. The combination of all three is outstanding and the dressing is lovely for any salad or baked or steamed vegetables.

SERVES 4 AS A SIDE SALAD

Trim the woody stems, if any, of the rocket. Toss the rocket, fennel and radicchio in a mixing bowl. Put the rest of the ingredients in a jar and shake. Pour the dressing over the salad and serve.

Variations

- If you're not avoiding dairy, you might add thinly shaved, really good quality Parmesan.
- A handful of semi-sundried tomatoes are a lovely addition.
- Add thinly sliced cucumber.
- Orange juice and/or segments go really well with fennel.
- Add one teaspoon of honey to the dressing.

Delicious dressings on all sorts of salads and vegetables enliven your tastebuds and add flavour. Here's a variety of dressings to try during summer.

2 TBSP BALSAMIC VINEGAR
1 TSP DIJON OR SEEDED MUSTARD
⅓ CUP FRESH ORANGE JUICE

1 TSP FRESH TARRAGON OR THYME LEAVES
SEA SALT AND PEPPER

Oil-free dressing [df, gf, vg, v]
MAKES ABOUT ½ CUP

Place all the ingredients in a jar with a lid. Shake well.

½ CUP FRESH ORANGE JUICE
2 LIMES, ZEST ONLY
1 TBSP EACH CORIANDER AND MINT LEAVES, FINELY SHREDDED

1 TBSP CUMIN SEEDS, TOASTED AND GROUND

Citrus dressing [df, gf, vg, v]
MAKES ABOUT ¾ CUP

Place all the ingredients in a jar with a lid. Shake well.

180 G FIRM TOFU (ONE SMALL PKT)
1 TBSP APPLE CIDER VINEGAR OR LEMON JUICE

1 TSP TAMARI OR SEA SALT
1 TBSP WATER

Tofu mayonnaise [df, gf, vg, v]
MAKES ABOUT 1 CUP

Place all ingredients in a processor and blend until smooth.

1 PIECE SPELT FLAT BREAD

1 TBSP OLIVE OIL

1 RED ONION, THINLY SLICED

1 TSP GROUND SUMAC

A HANDFUL EACH PARSLEY, CORIANDER
AND WATERCRESS LEAVES

1 CUP GOAT'S FETA, CRUMBLED

½ CUP WALNUTS, TOASTED

½ RED RADISH, THINLY SLICED

2 LEMONS, JUICED

OLIVE OIL

SEA SALT AND PEPPER

Herb salad *with* crisp bread, goat's feta, radish *and* walnuts [v]

This Lebanese-inspired salad is full of lemon juice and leafy greens to assist your liver. Sumac is the dried fruit of the bush with the same name, and it is ground to a tangy purple spice. I often serve this salad with pan-fried fish.

SERVES 4

Roll up the bread tightly and slice finely. Heat the oil in a pan and fry the bread until it turns golden. Remove from the pan and drain on absorbent paper.

Put the onion and sumac in a small bowl. Toss. Put the herbs, feta, walnuts, radish and fried bread in a separate bowl. Toss gently. Now mix everything together.

Finally, whisk together the lemon juice, olive oil and seasoning and pour over salad. Toss gently.

Use your fingers when adding salt to your food — your fingertips have 'memory', so they'll remember how much to add.

2 BIG HANDFULS OF EDIBLE FLOWERS
AND LEAVES LIKE NASTURTIUMS,
SORREL, CALENDULA, PANSY, RADISH
FLOWERS, VIOLETS, CHICORY LEAVES
AND DANDELION LEAVES

1 TBSP ORANGE JUICE

1 TSP ORANGE ZEST

1 TSP WHITE BALSAMIC VINEGAR

1 TBSP CAMELLIA OR SAFFLOWER OIL

1 TSP RAW HONEY

1 TSP SEA SALT

Nasturtium salad [*df, gf, vg, v*]

Edible flowers are lovely to add to salads, not just for their summery colours but also for their medicinal properties. Nasturtiums are high in iron; calendula is good for the lymph glands; radish is cooling; and dandelion leaves have a good effect on the kidney. Ask your green grocer to source them for you if you can't find them.

SERVES 2

Wash the flowers and leaves, dry well and put in a big bowl.
Put the rest of the ingredients in a jar and shake well to
combine. Pour over the salad and toss.

Sweet things

⅓ CUP RICE FLOUR

1½ CUPS ALMOND MILK

1 VANILLA POD, SPLIT AND SCRAPED

1 CUP WATER

¾ TSP AGAR AGAR FLAKES

3 TBSP DUTCH COCOA POWDER

⅓ CUP CAROB MOLASSES

2 TSP ORANGE ZEST OR ½ TSP ORANGE FLOWER WATER

COCOA POWDER, TO SERVE

Chocolate almond mousse
[df, gf, vg, v]

For chocolate lovers on a gluten-, dairy- and wheat-free diet, this mousse is a dream come true. I find that orange and chocolate make wonderful partners but you could leave the orange out if you don't agree. Buy the best quality cocoa you can find as it will make a real difference to the final taste. Agar agar is used instead of gelatin to set the dessert.

SERVES 4

Sift the flour into a pan and whisk in the almond milk. Add the seeds from the vanilla pod and bring to a simmer. Cook for about 5 minutes, stirring occasionally. It should start to glisten. Meanwhile, place the water and the agar agar in another pan, and simmer until the agar agar has dissolved, about two minutes. Add this to the flour and milk and stir well.

In a bowl combine the cocoa, molasses and orange zest to form a smooth paste. Pour into the flour and milk mixture in the pan and whisk well over a low heat to dissolve. Cool slightly, then pour into little bowls or pretty glasses and put in the fridge. They're ready to serve when the mousse is completely chilled. Serve with a sprinkling of cocoa powder.

4 RUBY GRAPEFRUIT

1 PUNNET STRAWBERRIES,
HALVED IF BIG

1 MANGO, CHEEKS QUARTERED

½ CUP COCONUT PALM SUGAR, GRATED

RICE OR SOY ICE CREAM

8 SKEWERS, SOAKED IN WATER

Fruit skewers [df, gf, vg, v]

I love easy desserts. Don't be afraid to use palm sugar as it tastes a bit like brown sugar but leans more towards caramel and butterscotch. Complex sweeteners such as this are actually recommended in the warmer months. Why not indulge yourself and marinate the fruit in a few tablespoons of Cointreau first?

MAKES 8 SKEWERS

Segment grapefruit (in fact, any citrus) by peeling and cutting away the pith first, then cutting the fruit into pieces so you will have nice nude segments with no white bits. Thread all the fruit onto skewers, alternating the varieties as you go. Grate a little palm sugar over the fruit then put the skewers on a barbecue or chargrill—under the grill of your oven will also work here. Cook the fruit quite quickly on both sides until golden brown and crunchy. Serve with rice or soy milk ice cream.

Variation

- Use halved fresh figs instead of grapefruit and strawberries.
- Substitute demura sugar for palm sugar.

4 BIG, JUICY, RIPE FIGS

1-2 TBSP BROWN SUGAR

1 CUP THICK, NATURAL YOGHURT

1 TBSP LEMON OR LIME ZEST

Caramelised figs [df, gf, v]

Figs are reputed to be an aphrodisiac and once you catch the scent of them coming off the grill, you'll be pretty happy you're about to eat them! With plump, juicy and delicious figs, there is something particularly luxurious about this dessert—even more so with a little Grand Marnier drizzled over the figs while still warm from the grill.

SERVES 4

Slice the figs in half then press them into the brown sugar. Place them face down straight onto a hot barbecue or chargrill and brown. Serve with a good dollop of yoghurt mixed with lemon zest.

Variations

- Drizzle some Grand Marnier over the figs as they come off the hotplate.
- Garnish with slithered almonds and berries.

2 TBSP RAW HONEY OR AGAVE OR MAPLE SYRUP

3 LIMES, JUICED

1 RIPE PAW PAW, SKINNED AND DE-SEEDED

2 TBSP SESAME SEEDS

Honeyed paw paw *with* sesame seeds [*df, gf, vg, v*]

Paw paw is one of those fruits that's too good to ignore. It's high in vitamin C and betacarotene and has reputed anti-cancer qualities. It has a different personality once mixed with the honey and lime and is also yummy inside Buckwheat and Coconut Pancakes (see page 101); topped with sheep's yoghurt; or on your morning cereal.

SERVES 4

Dissolve the honey and lime juice together—you may need to add a little hot water if you're using honey. Cut the paw paw into bite-sized chunks and put it in a bowl with the honey and lime dressing and the sesame seeds. Let it sit for a few minutes to allow the flavours to marry. The longer you let it sit the better it will be.

Variations

- Toss in half a cup of walnuts for extra crunch.
- This dish is great without the sweetener if you're watching your weight.
- Use orange instead of lime juice.
- Add half a cup LSA with or without the walnuts.

Drinks

---

2 CUPS FROZEN BERRIES

4 CUPS FRESH ORANGE JUICE

2 LIMES, JUICED

1 TBSP LIME ZEST

Berry *and* O.J. frappé [*df, gf, vg, v*]

Mixed berries look pretty and you can use any type you fancy. Blueberries are packed full of antioxidants and have been shown to slow down the ageing process and reduce the risk of developing Alzheimer's disease. It's also fine to buy your berries frozen as they retain most of their beneficial properties when frozen.

SERVES 4

Put all of the ingredients into a blender and blitz until smooth. Serve in four tall glasses.

Variations

- Add a frozen banana to the blender for a more substantial 'meal'.
- Adding a few mint leaves to the blender will give the drink a really fresh taste.

---

4 CUPS RAW OR COCONUT PALM SUGAR

2½ CUPS FILTERED WATER

1 TBSP LEMON JUICE

1 TSP ROSE WATER

2 TBSP GRENADINE

Rose water grenadine [*df, gf, vg, v*]

Make this gorgeous red syrup and have it in the fridge on standby. When ready, simply top it with mineral water for a great summer drink.

MAKES ABOUT 200ML

Place the sugar and water in a saucepan and bring to a slow simmer. Stir occasionally until the sugar dissolves. Add the lemon juice and simmer for another 10 minutes, without stirring. The lemon juice may create some froth; if so, skim it off.

Next, add the rose water and Grenadine, stir and simmer again for a couple of minutes. Take off the heat and cool slightly.

Pour into sterilised jars to cool completely. The syrup will keep in the fridge for a few months. To serve put about a tablespoon of the syrup in a glass and top with filtered water or sparkling mineral water.

---

1 DRAGONFRUIT

1–2 TBSP COCONUT PALM SUGAR, GRATED OR AGAVE SYRUP

1 TBSP LEMON JUICE

1 TBSP LEMON ZEST

3 CUPS SPARKLING MINERAL WATER

2 MINT LEAVES

ICE

2 DRAGONFUIT SLICES WITH SKIN ON, TO GARNISH

LEMON ZEST, TO GARNISH

Dragonfruit mocktail [df, gf, vg, v]

Dragonfruit is a tropical fruit with a spectacular bright red colour flecked with black. It has cooling properties due to its water content so it's perfect to serve on a hot summer's day.

SERVES 2

Halve the fruit and scoop the flesh into a bender, discarding the skin. Add all of the ingredients except the garnishes and blend. Serve in tall cocktail glasses with a slice of dragonfruit on the edge of the glass and the top of the drink sprinkled with a little lemon zest.

Autumn

The first time you feel that chill in the air is when you should start to think about *changing your shopping list* and what you've been cooking. As summer starts to fade *the call of autumn is in the air*. The leaves start to dry and fall, and a time of rest is approaching.

Object

Autumn is about nurturing and supporting your organs and building your blood in preparation for winter.

Organ

This is the season when your lungs and colon are in the spotlight. They are both eliminatory channels, which mean they help you 'let go' both physically and emotionally.

Emotion

The emotions stored in these organs are grief and sadness. Unresolved emotions will eventually present as physical symptoms.

Symptoms

This is the time when coughs, breathing difficulties and other respiratory disorders appear, as do gastrointestinal complaints like loose stools and/or constipation. These symptoms are telling you it's time to 'let go'.

Flavour & foods

- Pungent flavours are most associated with autumn. This means you need to include foods like ginger, garlic, wasabi and coriander in your diet now.
- You'll also want to include foods that will moisten your body, such as soy products; vegetables like mushrooms, leeks, sweet potato, carrots, zucchini, English and baby spinach and cabbage; sea vegetables; fruit such as apples, olives, figs, grapes, pears, persimmons; fresh and roasted nuts like almonds, organic peanuts and pine nuts; and grains like barley, rice and millet; and sourdough and toasted rye bread.
- Legumes like adzuki, borlotti, kidney and lima beans, and herbs like spearmint and peppermint are perfect at this time of year.
- Seafood for autumn includes clams and fish stocks.

- Think also organic chicken broth, yoghurt and eggs, and all types of vinegar.
- Sour foods like lemon, lime and grapefruit will also be of help during autumn.
- It's a good idea to eat a little more of good quality oils—that doesn't (and never does) mean refined or processed fats and oils but oils, in foods like avocado, nuts and seeds, tahini, olive and flax.
- The wind tends to dry us out at this time—our lips chap, and we have dry coughs and skin. The condition of your skin reflects the state of your lungs, so protect them by keeping your skin moist.

Cooking methods

Steaming and boiling are appropriate now, although towards the end of autumn, start roasting and making casseroles, dahls and stews as well. This is the season to make your own stock and eat lots of soups. The aim is to build up your blood so it keeps you warm during winter.

Avoid

Some immunity is lost through your skin, so avoid too many heating spices like chillies and hot paprika. Also avoid cold foods, drinks, salads and juices as these direct energy inwards and make it contract. Raw onions should be reduced too. Avoid cooking quickly as you would in summer. Now is the season for slow cooking—take your time in the kitchen and enjoy the reduced pace.

Fresh in autumn

Fruit: apple / banana / feijoa / fig / grape / guava / kiwifruit / lemon / lime / mangosteen / nectarine / orange / papaya / passionfruit / peach / pear / persimmon / plum / pomegranate / rambutan / avocado / cumquat / custard apple / mandarin / quince / beetroot / tomato

Vegetables: Asian greens / bean / capsicum / celery / chilli / cucumber / daikon / eggplant / leek / lettuce / okra / brown onion / spring onion / olive / green pea / potato / pumpkin / shallot / silver beet / spinach / squash / sweetcorn / sweet potato / zucchini / broccoli / Brussel sprout / cabbage / carrot / cauliflower / fennel / garlic / ginger / mushroom / parsnip / horseradish / swede

Seafood: Atlantic salmon / yellow fin bream / tiger flathead / southern garfish / ocean jacket / sea mullet / King George whiting / blue swimmer crab / mud crab / Sydney rock oyster / king prawn / school prawn / tiger prawn / squid

Breakfast

1 CUP WHITE OR WHOLEMEAL
SPELT FLOUR

1½ CUPS BUCKWHEAT FLOUR

1 TSP GROUND CINNAMON

PINCH SEA SALT

½ CUP SHREDDED COCONUT

2 FREE-RANGE EGGS

¼ CUP LIGHT OIL LIKE SAFFLOWER OR
SUNFLOWER, PLUS EXTRA FOR COOKING

300 ML SOY, QUINOA OR
ALMOND MILK

SAFFLOWER OIL, FOR COOKING

Buckwheat *and* coconut pancakes [*df, v*]

Traditionally, crepes and pancakes are made with white flour, sugar and butter. This version is not so different but much healthier. Sweeten up the pancakes if you like by adding some real maple syrup or agave. These are absolutely delicious for breakfast or dessert.

MAKES ABOUT 8 PANCAKES

Sift flours, cinnamon and salt in a bowl and then add coconut. In a separate bowl beat together the eggs, oil and milk and slowly add the mixture to the dry ingredients, whisking after each addition until all is added and you have a smooth batter.

Heat a pan over a medium heat and add a little oil. You can use olive oil spray or a paper towel to reduce the amount you use. Pour in a small amount of batter, about a quarter of a cup, and swirl so the batter is evenly spread in the pan. Turn the pancake when bubbles appear on surface—about 1 minute, depending on thickness—then cook on the other side until golden.

Variations

- Fill the crepes with Honeyed Paw Paw (*see page 93*), Hazelnut sauce (*see page 158*) and chocolate sauce or simply serve with fresh lemon and agave.
- For gluten-free pancakes, substitute the spelt flour with buckwheat, brown rice or besan flour.
- Camellia or grape seed oils or Omega spread are also good oil choices.

1 TSP OLIVE OIL

1 TSP GROUND TURMERIC

2 CUPS BUTTON OR FIELD MUSHROOMS, SLICED

1 GARLIC CLOVE, CRUSHED

180 G (6 oz) SOFT TOFU, CRUMBLED

1 TBSP TAMARI

1 HANDFUL EACH OF PARSLEY AND BASIL, SHREDDED

CRACKED BLACK PEPPER

2 BIG HANDFULS ROCKET OR BABY OR ENGLISH SPINACH, ROUGHLY CHOPPED

4 SLICES RYE SOURDOUGH OR FLATBREAD

Scrambled tofu *and* mushrooms [df, vg, v]

Eating protein for breakfast is a good way to keep sugar cravings at bay for the rest of the day. As tofu is full of protein, low in fat and a complex carbohydrate, it will keep your blood sugar stable for hours and aid your brain function. This delicious recipe is great way to start the day.

SERVES 4

In a heavy-based pan, heat the olive oil then add the turmeric. Stir for about 30 seconds before adding the mushrooms and garlic. Cook until mushrooms start to soften—you may need to add a dash of water to get them cooking. Add the tofu and stir over a fairly high heat for about 2 minutes. When heated through, add the Tamari, herbs and pepper.

Turn the heat off and stir through the rocket or spinach. Put a lid on so the greens wilt. Serve on the sourdough or wrap in the flatbread. Yum!

Variations

- A dash of fish sauce will make the dish saltier and more like an Asian stir-fry.
- If you're on the Asian theme, also add a couple of teaspoons of grated ginger with the garlic and/or a few drops of sesame oil.
- For the herbs, toss in a handful of coriander leaves instead of the basil.
- Add two teaspoons of finely chopped coriander stems and roots with the oil.
- Any vegetable you like can be mixed in with the mushrooms. Try corn, chopped zucchini and julienne carrots as they all work beautifully.

2 CUPS ORGANIC ROLLED OATS

3 CUPS SUGAR-FREE ORANGE, APPLE OR PEAR JUICE

½–1 CUP YOGHURT

½ CUP ALMONDS

½ CUP APPLE, GRATED

½ CUP SHREDDED COCONUT

½ CUP SULTANAS OR CURRANTS

2 TBSP LEMON OR LIME ZEST

YOGHURT, TO SERVE

Bircher muesli [v]

Bircher has been a favourite of the health conscious for a long time—for good reason. Some grains, like oats, are difficult to digest, but soaking them overnight increases their digestibility. You can treat other grains, nuts and seeds in the same way to soften them.

SERVES 4

Cover the oats with the juice and let soak overnight in the fridge. In the morning, mix the yoghurt through so the mixture has the consistency of cake batter. Roast the almonds on an oven tray at 180°C (350°F) for 20 minutes or until you can smell their gorgeous scent. Let cool, then chop roughly. Mix the almonds, apple, coconut and sultanas through the oats. Serve topped with the zest and yoghurt.

Variations

- You can buy almonds already roasted; just ensure they are 'dry-roasted'.
- Top your muesli with roasted pepitas, LSA or stewed rhubarb.

4 CUPS ORGANIC RAW OATS

1 CUP CHOPPED OR
SLITHERED ALMONDS

1 CUP SESAME SEEDS

1 CUP SUNFLOWER SEEDS

1 CUP PEPITAS

1 TBSP GROUND CINNAMON

½ CUP SPELT FLOUR

½ CUP AGAVE, PEAR OR APPLE JUICE
CONCENTRATE OR MAPLE SYRUP,
OR TO TASTE

½ CUP OMEGA SPREAD OR CAMELLIA OIL

Toasted muesli [*df, vg, v*]

Commercially produced toasted muesli is often full of refined fats, sodium and sugar but this one is full of goodness with all the tastes you'll love. Those who make their own muesli will tell you about the satisfaction they get from doing so. You can get creative with your ingredients; my list above is merely a guide to get you started.

10 TO 12 SERVES

Mix all the dry ingredients together in a large bowl. Combine the sweetener and Omega spread or oil separately. Using your hands, rub the liquid through the dry ingredients, keeping it a little chunky. Spread the mixture on a baking tray and toast in the oven at 180°C (350°F) until brown and crispy—about 20 minutes—turning once. Cool, then store in an airtight container.

Variations

- Mix a cup of organic dried fruit through the muesli after baking.
- Add a cup of LSA after baking.
- Use quinoa flakes instead of oats, or try a half/half combination.
- Rolled brown rice may be used instead of oats.
- For a raw muesli, omit the sweetener and Omega spread and don't cook.
- Add a cup of bran for extra roughage when you mix the dry ingredients.
- To make a crumble, stew some fruit, pop it in a baking dish, top with some pre-baked muesli then cook in the oven.
- Try another type of oil like grapeseed or safflower for a different flavour.

½ CUP WHITE VINEGAR

2 TSP SEA SALT

4 FREE-RANGE EGGS

4 PIECES OF ESSENE BREAD

4 SLICES SMOKED SALMON

1 LEMON, QUARTERED

LARGE HANDFUL PARSLEY OR BABY CRESS

CRACKED PEPPER

Essene bread *with* poached egg *and* smoked salmon [*df*]

Due to the oil in salmon, this is a great dish to have in autumn. It is also a good meal in early spring, as sprouts are idea foods for that season. Essene bread is a sprouted grain bread, which is incredibly high in available nutrients. Its texture is dense and it tastes a little nutty, a bit like pumpernickel.

SERVES 4

Fill a deep pot with water, add the vinegar and salt and put it on the stovetop to heat. Wait until the water reaches a gentle simmer, then swirl it around to create a bit of a whirlpool. Crack the eggs and drop them into the water—the swirling action will allow the egg white to wrap around the yolk so you get a nicely-shaped poached egg. Let the eggs cook for about a minute then remove them with a slotted spoon onto a piece of paper towel to drain any excess water. You'll know they're cooked when they are white and a little firm, but not hard.

Place a piece of toasted bread on four separate plates, top with the salmon and then gently place an egg on each serve. Place the lemon on the side and pile fresh parsley or baby cress high on top of each serving. Season with cracked pepper.

Variation

- Top each piece of bread with a quarter of an avocado. Gently lay an egg on top of the avocado, then the salmon. Use half a cup of Tahini Dressing (*see page 149*) to finish.

8 PORTOBELLO MUSHROOMS,
OR 4 IF THEY'RE ESPECIALLY LARGE

1 CLOVE GARLIC, CHOPPED
OR SQUASHED

1 TBSP OLIVE OIL

2 TSP SEA SALT AND CRACKED PEPPER

2 TBSP TAHINI DRESSING (*See page 149*)

1 TBSP FRESH MINT
AND/OR PARSLEY, SHREDDED

Grilled mushrooms *with* tahini dressing [*df, gf, vg, v*]

Mushrooms are loaded with protein and fibre and are always lovely for breakfast. The dressing gives you the extra good oil you need in autumn to protect your skin and keep your digestive tract lubricated.

SERVES 4

Rub the mushrooms with the garlic, drizzle with the oil then place on a tray. Sprinkle with salt and pepper and grill until soft—about 5 minutes. Drizzle with the Tahini Dressing and sprinkle with chopped herbs.

Variations

- Sprinkle with a couple of teaspoons of fresh or dried thyme or oregano instead of mint and parsley.
- Serve on toasted spelt or rye sourdough or wrap up in mountain bread.
- Top with fresh baby spinach.

Don't be concerned about the fat in avocado, tahini, nuts and seeds, etc., as it's good fat and we need it. Bad fats, like those from an animal, you should avoid.

Lunch

---

2 LITRES FISH STOCK

4 SPRING ONIONS, WHITE PART ONLY, CHOPPED

2 TBSP OLIVE OIL

2 GARLIC CLOVES, CRUSHED

1 CUP ARBORIO RICE OR ORGANIC BROWN RICE

2 PIECES OF SNAPPER, CUT INTO BITE-SIZED CHUNKS

¾ CUP PEAS

½ CUP PARSLEY, CHOPPED

Snapper *and* pea risotto [*df, gf*]

It's okay to eat risotto occasionally, especially if it's for lunch when you have the afternoon to work it off. Don't go overboard and eat piles of it—it'll go straight to your waistline if you do. But it really is a lovely dish and one to enjoy every now and then.

SERVES 4

Simmer the stock in a saucepan. In another saucepan, slowly sauté the onions in the olive oil with the garlic. Add the rice and stir until the rice becomes translucent. Add enough of the simmering stock to cover the rice and stir until it has absorbed. Add more stock and continue cooking and adding in this manner until the rice is al dente.

Add the fish to the risotto with the peas and half the parsley. Stir for another minute, remove from heat then let sit for a few minutes with the lid on. The rice should be wet/sloppy. Stir and serve from the pan, garnished with a little more parsley.

Variations

- Instead of spring onions you could use one onion or leek, finely chopped.
- Use brown rice or barley instead of the arborio rice.
- Half a cup of white wine added along with the stock will make it extra yummy.
- Stir through a cup of lightly steamed beetroot cubes just before serving.
- Try different vegetables like corn, mushrooms or asparagus, with or without the peas—you might need to add vegies like corn a little earlier to allow them to cook through.
- Porcini mushrooms make this dish especially delicious.
- Add a tablespoon of lemon zest towards the end for zing.
- A splash of umeboshi vinegar just before serving will give it an extra lift.
- Add two anchovies to the onions.

500 G (1 lb 2 oz) FLATHEAD OR REDFISH, CHOPPED

1 TBSP GREEN CURRY PASTE

1 CUP GREEN BEANS, CHOPPED

2 FRESH KAFFIR LIME LEAVES, SLICED

2 TBSP CORIANDER ROOTS, STEMS AND LEAVES, FINELY CHOPPED

1 FREE-RANGE EGG

1 TSP SEA SALT OR FISH SAUCE

OLIVE, CAMELLIA, SAFFLOWER OR ORGANIC PEANUT OIL, FOR FRYING

Dressing

3 SPRING ONIONS, WHITE PART ONLY, FINELY CHOPPED

¼ CUP BROWN RICE OR WHITE WINE VINEGAR

⅓ CUP WATER

1 TBSP COCONUT PALM SUGAR, GRATED

1 RED CHILLI, FINELY CHOPPED

1 TSP FISH SAUCE

Thai fish cakes [df, gf]

This is an easy and tasty recipe, which I make often. Your kids will love these fish cakes. It is a good way to include fish in your diet and you won't get those fishy smells in the kitchen with this recipe. The cakes freeze well so make double quantity and pop the unused mixture into the freezer until you're ready to use it.

MAKES ABOUT 20

For the fish cakes, put all the ingredients except the oil in a food processor and blend to a paste. Roll the mixture into balls—wet hands will make this easier—then flatten into cakes. Heat the oil in a shallow pan and fry the fish cakes until golden brown on one side, then flip and cook the other side until golden brown.

For the dressing, place all the ingredients in a small saucepan and heat. Stir until the sugar has dissolved then simmer for a few minutes. Leave to cool. Serve the dressing at room temperature or chilled.

Variations

- Add a tablespoon of grated ginger to the fish cake mixture.
- Add two cloves of garlic to give extra piquancy.
- If you use dried lime leaves, soak them for 10 minutes then slice and use.

8 ASIAN/LONG EGGPLANT (TO YIELD 4 CUPS)

4 TBSP OLIVE OIL

1 LARGE LEEK, HALVED AND CLEANED

2 CLOVES GARLIC, CRUSHED

1 GREEN CHILLI, CHOPPED

1 TBSP GINGER, FINELY SLICED

1 TBSP CORIANDER STEMS, FINELY CHOPPED

3–4 SACHETS DASHI

1 TSP SESAME OIL

2 TSP TAMARI

2 PKT SILKEN TOFU, CUT INTO LARGE SQUARES

4 SPRING ONIONS, SLICED ON THE DIAGONAL

2 TBSP CORIANDER LEAVES

Chinese eggplant *with* tofu *and* ginger [*df, gf*]

This recipe was inspired by something similar that my sister Marisa had in a Chinese restaurant in Sydney, and she set out to recreate it. Between the two of us I think we've come up with a divine dish. It is one of my top-five favourite dishes in the cooler months. It's not only my Monday and Tuesday and whenever lunch, it's my Sunday night comfort food too.

SERVES 4

Slice the eggplants into wedges of approximately four centimetres long. Lightly fry them in half the oil until they start to brown all over—eggplant soaks up oil so you may need to add more. If you want to avoid using too much, brush the eggplant with oil and grill or bake it. Remove from pan and place on a paper towel.

Slice leek into half moons and place in the same pan with the rest of the oil. Cook over medium heat, adding garlic, chilli, ginger and coriander stems and cook for a minute. Add the eggplant with enough water to cover, and then add the dashi, sesame oil and Tamari. Let simmer until the eggplant is soft and tender, about 15 minutes.

Gently add the tofu to the pan to warm through—do be gentle as silken tofu falls apart easily. Serve garnished with spring onions and coriander leaves.

Variations

- This is nice served with quinoa or organic brown rice.
- Add fresh or dried shiitake mushrooms with the dashi, keeping them whole and allowing two per person.
- Organic chicken goes really well with this—brown the chicken pieces first in oil, then drain and add them with the dashi. Use the same oil to sauté the leeks.
- Brown some chopped green capsicum with the eggplant.

1 CUP BROWN OR GREEN LENTILS,
PAR-COOKED

12–16 SAVOY CABBAGE OR LARGE
SILVERBEET LEAVES

1 CUP ORGANIC, SHORT GRAIN
BROWN RICE, PAR-COOKED

1 CUP QUINOA

1 CUP PINE NUTS

2 TSP GROUND CUMIN

2 TSP SWEET PAPRIKA

1 TBSP SEA SALT

1 HANDFUL EACH MINT AND PARSLEY,
SHREDDED

400 G CAN WHOLE PEELED TOMATOES

1 CUP WATER

Cabbage rolls [df, gf, vg, v]

My mum used to make massive pots of these when we were children. I guess it made sense to cook in bulk as she had four hungry children to feed, and very often many of their equally ravenous friends as well. She used to make the rolls in the traditional Lebanese way with lamb, white rice and of course garlic. This is my version.

SERVES 4

Soak the lentils overnight then drain. Heat a large pot of water. Blanch the cabbage leaves one at a time, until they are soft enough to roll but not soggy. Set aside and let cool. Meanwhile, combine the rest of the ingredients in a bowl, except the tomatoes and water.

Lay one cabbage leaf on a dry surface and fill with about a tablespoon of the mixture. Roll up, tucking in the ends as you go—don't roll them too tightly as the stuffing will expand as the rice and lentils finish cooking. Repeat with the remaining leaves and pack them into a saucepan as you go.

Pour the tomatoes and water over the rolls. Heat and let them simmer for about 30 minutes.

Variations

• You can use canned lentils instead of dried. Cooking time will halve.
• Try adding different spices like allspice and turmeric to the mixture.
• Two or three crushed garlic cloves add great flavour.
• Add one tablespoon of tomato paste to the pot.

Lime and wasabi dressing

2 TBSP OLIVE OIL

2 TBSP LIME JUICE

1–2 TSP TAMARI

1 GARLIC CLOVE, CRUSHED

1 TSP WASABI PASTE

2 DESIREE OR PONTIAC POTATOES

2 FREE-RANGE EGGS

1 CUP PARSLEY, CHOPPED

2 PIECES FRESH TUNA

2 TBSP OLIVE OIL

2 HANDFULS GREEN BEANS, TOPPED
THEN LIGHTLY BLANCHED OR STEAMED

1 FENNEL BULB, TRIMMED THEN SLICED
WITH EITHER A MANDOLIN,
KNIFE OR PEELER

2 SPRING ONIONS, FINELY CHOPPED

4 BIG HANDFULS ROCKET OR
BABY SPINACH

1 CUP EXTRA PARSLEY, CHOPPED

CRACKED PEPPER

1 LEMON OR LIME, QUARTERED

Niçoise salad [df, gf]

This is not your everyday Niçoise—it's even more delicious. Even though we're sometimes told potatoes are bad for us, they're not. Just be mindful not to eat them every day—everything in moderation. The red varieties like pontiac and desiree are less inflammatory than others, and even less so if you add miso paste or sea salt to them.

SERVES 4

To make the dressing, place all the ingredients in a jar and shake well. For the salad, boil the potatoes until just tender and then chop into large chunks and let cool. Boil the eggs for four minutes only—they still need to be a bit runny.

Press the chopped parsley into the tuna pieces. Heat the oil in a pan and when it is quite hot add the tuna—this will create lots of smoke, so an exhaust fan is helpful, or cook outside on the barbecue. Cook for about 30 seconds on each side, so the tuna is just changing colour on the outside and is still pink inside. Let it rest while you're making the salad.

Gently combine the spuds, beans, fennel, spring onions, greens and extra parsley and pour over about three-quarters of the dressing. Divide the salad between four plates or lay on one large platter. Finely slice the tuna into centimetre-long strips and halve the eggs. Arrange the tuna and eggs on top of the salad and drizzle the remaining dressing over the tuna and egg. Garnish with cracked pepper, fresh lemon or lime quarters.

Pomegranate dressing

1 TBSP RED WINE VINEGAR

1 TSP POMEGRANATE MOLASSES

3 TBSP OLIVE OIL

1 SHALLOT, FINELY DICED

1 GARLIC CLOVE, CRUSHED

1 TBSP FRESH THYME LEAVES

PINCH SEA SALT

1 FENNEL BULB, QUARTERED

1-2 TBSP OLIVE OIL

1 TSP SEA SALT

1 CAN CANNELLINI BEANS

1 BUNCH ROCKET, TRIMMED AND ROUGHLY CHOPPED

SEEDS OF 1 POMEGRANATE

Fennel *and* pomegranate salad [*df, gf, vg, v*]

Pomegranate is highly prized for its medicinal properties in India. It's reputed to reduce phlegm so it's a wonderful ingredient to include in the cooler months when colds and flus are common. The fennel goes with it beautifully and aids digestion, which will help with weight loss, again wonderful for the cooler months.

SERVES 2

For the dressing, in a little bowl whisk together the vinegar and molasses until combined, then whisk in the oil. Add the rest of the ingredients. Put in a jar and set aside for as long as possible so the flavours integrate.

Put the fennel on a baking tray and drizzle with olive oil and sea salt. Bake at 180°C until soft, about 20 minutes. Cool a little then place on a platter. In a bowl gently toss together the beans, rocket and pomegranate seeds, then add the dressing. Spoon this over the fennel.

2½ CUPS WATER

1 CUP ORGANIC SHORT-GRAIN
BROWN RICE

1 TSP MIRIN (*optional*)

1 TBSP RICE WINE VINEGAR (*optional*)

4 SHEETS NORI

2 TBSP SOY MAYONNAISE

1 AVOCADO, THINLY SLICED

½ BLOCK YUMMY TOFU (*see page 154*)

1 SMALL CUCUMBER, DE-SEEDED
AND THINLY SLICED

4 SPRING ONIONS, CLEANED AND SLICED
ONCE LENGTHWAYS

½ CUP TAMARI

1 TSP SESAME OIL

Nori rolls [*df, gf, vg, v*]

Nori rolls are very popular and most of us think we're eating a healthy food when we buy them from a sushi bar. The problem is that the white rice used in most of the rolls is excessively refined, with white sugar added as well. Nori is good for you, as are all sea vegetables, and it would be a shame to stop eating it because of the rice. So make your own with brown rice! These rolls are fabulous to take to work or school for lunch; beautiful cut into two-centimetre-thick pieces and served with the sauce as an hors d'oeuvre; and great to have on hand as a tasty snack for you and the kids.

MAKES 4 LONG ROLLS

Boil the water then add the rice. When cooked—the water should be fully absorbed by the rice—put it into a bowl and stir through the mirin and vinegar if using. Let it cool completely.

Prepare the nori sheets as per the instructions on the packet. Place a sheet of nori on a clean, dry surface or a bamboo mat suitable for rolling. Using slightly wet hands, gently press about half a cup of rice onto the nori sheet—it should be about a centimetre thick—leaving about a centimetre along the edge of the sheet free of rice. Smear the rice with some mayo, then add avocado, tofu, cucumber and spring onions.

Using your hands or the bamboo mat, roll the nori up evenly—be careful as it will burst if there's too much rice or filling. Repeat with the remaining nori sheets and ingredients and . . . it's ready to eat!

Variations

- Mix drained tuna with a little soy mayonnaise instead of the tofu—you can do this with shredded, cooked, organic chicken or sashimi-grade tuna or salmon too.
- Adding carrot sticks gives the rolls a nice crunch.
- Mix together ½ cup Tahini Dressing (*see page 149*), a teaspoon of white miso paste and one teaspoon Tamari and then mix with 1 cup steamed white fish like flathead. Roll up in the nori sheets with rice and chopped spring onions and/or coriander leaves and stems.

1 SMALL LEEK, WHITE PART ONLY,
WASHED AND CHOPPED FINELY

2 GARLIC CLOVES, CHOPPED

2 TBSP OLIVE OIL

4 CUPS BROCCOLI FLORETS, CHOPPED

1 SMALL RED CAPSICUM, DICED
AND DE-SEEDED

1 TBSP FRESH DILL, CHOPPED

2½ LITRES STOCK, PREFERABLY
HOME-MADE

4 LARGE FREE-RANGE EGGS

½ CUP LEMON JUICE

1 CUP BIODYNAMIC SHORT-GRAIN
BROWN RICE, COOKED

FRESH PARSLEY, TO GARNISH

Broccoli egg-lemon soup [df, gf, v]

The flavour and generous helpings of broccoli in this recipe suggests spring to me, but this soup is suitable for slightly warmer weather. So you can consider this one an autumn pleasure or make it when you feel like soup on those cooler days in spring or summer.

SERVES 4

Sauté the leek and garlic in the olive oil until translucent. Add the broccoli, capsicum (leave out if you have any inflammatory conditions), dill and two litres of the stock and bring to a simmer. Meanwhile, whisk together the eggs, lemon juice and remaining half cup of stock in a bowl. When the vegies are just cooked, gradually pour the egg mixture into the soup while stirring. Lastly, add the rice and re-heat the soup gently—don't boil it. Serve in bowls and garnish with parsley.

*To make your own stock —it's so worth it —
keep all your vegetable scraps in a freezer bag and when ready,
simmer them in a large pot for about an hour, then strain.
Store in the freezer so it's available when you need it.*

1 LEEK, WHITE PART ONLY, WASHED AND CHOPPED

2 TBSP OLIVE OIL

2 CLOVES GARLIC, CHOPPED

4 CUPS ASSORTED MUSHROOMS, CHOPPED

1 LITRE VEGETABLE STOCK

1 TBSP SAGE OR THYME LEAVES, CHOPPED

SEA SALT AND CRACKED PEPPER

1 CUP ITALIAN PARSLEY

180 G (6 oz) SILKEN TOFU

Mushroom *and* tofu soup [df, gf, vg, v]

Lots of people are fond of creamy soups and there is no reason to go without with this wonderful recipe. If you're dairy-free or watching your weight and cholesterol, using silken tofu instead of the cream that normally goes into many soups is the way to go. The end result won't taste exactly the same but I think it's better, especially for those who care about their arteries. I couldn't eat a bowl of soup with cream anymore—it would just be too rich, and my gallbladder would be most unhappy.

SERVES 4

Sauté the leek in oil until soft then add the garlic and mushrooms and give it a good stir. Add the stock, herbs and seasoning and bring to the boil. Let simmer until the mushrooms are soft—this should take about 15 minutes, but the longer you leave it simmering the nicer the end result will be.

Put half the soup in a blender—or put a hand-held stick blender straight into the pot—with the parsley and process until smooth. Add the tofu and process again. Pour this puree back into the soup pot. Mix and taste for seasoning. Serve with cracked pepper and top with some extra fresh sage leaves and/or Italian parsley.

Variations

- Add a spoonful (or scoop) of organic brown rice to the bowls before the soup goes in for a fuller meal.
- Finish with a splash of umeboshi vinegar for extra health benefits and extra zing.
- Add a couple of potatoes to the pot with the mushrooms—this will make the soup even creamier.
- Add a cup of soy or almond milk just before serving to make it even richer.

8 GREEN PRAWNS, SHELLED,
DE-VEINED AND ROUGHLY CHOPPED

1 LARGE FLATHEAD OR ANOTHER FIRM
FISH LIKE REDFISH OR SNAPPER,
ROUGHLY CHOPPED, FILLETED AND
SKINNED

1–2 GARLIC CLOVES, CRUSHED

1 TSP GINGER, GRATED

1 TSP SESAME OIL

2 SPRING ONIONS, ROUGHLY CHOPPED

SMALL HANDFUL EACH CORIANDER
LEAVES AND PARSLEY, CHOPPED

2 FREE-RANGE EGGS

1 TBSP LIME OR LEMON JUICE
AND A LITTLE OF THE RIND, ZESTED

2 TBSP SPELT BREADCRUMBS OR
SPELT FLOUR

SEA SALT AND PEPPER, TO TASTE

1 PKT OF QUINOA UDON, BUCKWHEAT
OR KAMUT NOODLES

2½ LITRES FISH OR CHICKEN STOCK

TAMARI SEEDS (*see page 146*),
TO GARNISH

BEAN SPROUTS, TO GARNISH

SLICED SPRING ONION, TO GARNISH

CORIANDER LEAVES, TO GARNISH

Seafood ball soup *with* quinoa noodles [*df*]

I love this soup. It's clear, thin and very tasty. It has everything: a slurp of quinoa noodles, a little bite of seafood and some crunch from the sprouts and the seeds. It also tastes wonderful without the noodles if you're watching your weight or avoiding carbs. If that's the case, you might toss in a big handful of English spinach.

SERVES 4

Place all ingredients except the noodles, stock and garnishes in a food processor to combine. If possible, refrigerate mixture for about 30 minutes. Remove from refrigerator and with wet hands, roll into balls, using about one to two tablespoons of the mixture for each ball—you should have about 12 balls. Put them on a tray and pop them back in the refrigerator until you are ready to cook.

Cook the noodles according to the packet instructions. While the noodles are cooking, carefully place the balls into simmering stock and cook for about three minutes, or until opaque—they will float on the surface of the stock when ready.

Divide the noodles evenly between four soup bowls. Using a slotted spoon, put four balls in each bowl. Pour stock over and garnish with Tamari Seeds, bean sprouts, sliced spring onions and coriander leaves. A wedge of lime is a sexy addition.

Dinner

---

4 CUPS KUMERA
1 TBSP OLIVE OIL
2 TSP CHILLI POWDER
1 TBSP ASAFOETIDA
1 TBSP GARAM MASALA
1 TBSP LEMON OR LIME JUICE

1 CUP COCONUT FLAKES
1 BUNCH CORIANDER LEAVES, ROUGHLY CHOPPED
⅓ CUP TOASTED SESAME SEEDS
½ CUP ORGANIC DRY ROASTED PEANUTS

Kumera salad [df, gf, vg, v]

Everyone loves this salad—not only because of the wonderful flavours, but because it's so simple to make. The sesame seeds are a good source of calcium, fibre and essential fatty acids, and toasting them really brings out their nutty flavour. You may not have used asafoetida before but do try it. It's a great herb that very handily replaces garlic and onions. Beware, it tastes better than it smells in the bottle.

SERVES 4

Chop kumera into large, even chunks and steam until tender but not mushy. Heat the oil in a pan and add the spices, frying until fragrant. Pour the oil over the warm kumera. Let cool then add the citrus juice. Next, toss through the coconut flakes, coriander leaves, sesame seeds and peanuts.

(see photo page 124)

4 FIRM WHITE FISH FILLETS
LIKE FLATHEAD, COD OR SNAPPER

1 CUP WATER

4 TBSP SHAO HSING WINE
OR DRY SHERRY

4 TBSP TAMARI

1 TSP SESAME OIL

4 TBSP GINGER, JULIENNED

4 SPRING ONIONS, JULIENNED

2 CHINESE CABBAGE LEAVES

1 CUP CORIANDER LEAVES

1 TSP GROUND WHITE PEPPER

Oriental steamed fish [df, gf]

This is one of my favourite dishes—it looks and smells wonderful and when it's a little cooler outside, you can just feel the warmth of the ginger doing you good. If you don't have a steamer, then just place all the ingredients in a shallow pan. It is perfect when served with biodynamic steamed brown rice or quinoa noodles and Asian greens.

SERVES 4

Cut the fish into big chunks. Place in a ceramic bowl that will fit inside a bamboo steamer. Pour the water, wine, Tamari, sesame oil and half the ginger and spring onions over the fish.
Place the bowl inside the steamer in a wok or pan that is less than half full of boiling water. Cover and steam for 5 to 6 minutes. Then place the cabbage inside the steamer on top of the fish. Cover again and steam for a further few minutes, until the cabbage has softened and the fish is cooked—the flesh should break away easily when prodded with a fork.

Place the cabbage on a large serving platter and top with the fish. Pour the liquid in the bowl gently over the fish then garnish with the remaining ginger, spring onions, coriander leaves and pepper.

Variations

- You can add all sorts of different spices to this dish, so try five spice, Szechuan pepper or chilli for a different taste.
- Add wood or fungus to the fish when steaming.

2 FREE-RANGE EGGS

½ CUP SPELT OR RICE FLOUR

SEA SALT AND CRACKED PEPPER

4 FIRM WHITE FISH FILLETS LIKE
BLUE-EYE TREVALLA, FLATHEAD,
SNAPPER, GEMFISH OR JEWFISH

1 CUP SPELT BREADCRUMBS

2 TBSP OLIVE OIL

1 LEMON, CUT INTO WEDGES

CHOPPED PARSLEY, TO GARNISH

Spelt-crumbed fish fingers [*df*]

Lots of people say they don't cook fish because they don't know how to keep it moist and flavour-some. Try this recipe, which is especially good for children who love fish fingers. You won't go wrong, and once you've made it you'll feel confident to experiment with the variations.

SERVES 4

Beat the eggs in a bowl. Place the flour on a flat plate and season. Place the breadcrumbs on another plate. Cut the fish into fingers about three centimetres wide. Coat the fish in the flour, then the egg and then the breadcrumbs.

Add the oil to a hot pan and pop the fish in. Pan-fry the fish for about one minute, or until golden brown, then turn over. Cook the other side the same way. Take the fish out and drain on absorbent paper. Serve with lemon and parsley.

Variations

- Season flour with ground spices like turmeric, cumin powder, Cajun spice mix, garam masala, panch phoron or sesame seeds.
- Rub fish with a little shiro miso paste or pesto before coating with flour.
- Coat the fish with the flour only, omitting egg and breadcrumbs.
- Add finely chopped fresh herbs like coriander, mint and/or parsley to the flour or breadcrumbs and use with or without the egg.
- Use LSA mix or almond instead of the flour to make a GF version.

1 LITRE FILTERED WATER

3 SACHETS DASHI POWDER
OR 1 LITRE FISH STOCK

1 TBSP GINGER, FINELY SLICED OR
GRATED

1 BUNCH CORIANDER STEMS, FINELY
CHOPPED

8 FRESH SHIITAKE MUSHROOMS, SLICED

2 TSP SESAME OIL

2 TBSP ARAME OR ONE STICK KOMBU

4 BLUE-EYE TREVALLA FILLETS OR
CUTLETS

1 CUP CORIANDER LEAVES, FINELY
CHOPPED

4 TBSP SPRING ONIONS, FINELY SLICED

Poached trevalla *in* Asian broth [*df, gf*]

This is a really lovely, nourishing broth, and it's bound to become a staple once you've tried it. Silken tofu, organic chicken or duck may be used instead of the fish.

SERVES 4

Put the water, dashi, ginger, coriander, mushrooms, oil and arame in a large skillet or frying pan and let it simmer for at least 10 minutes. Add the fish and poach for about 3 minutes or until it is opaque and tender. Serve in shallow bowls garnished with chopped coriander leaves and spring onions.

Variations

- If using dried shiitake mushrooms, pull them out of the stock once they are soft and de-stem and slice finely before putting them back into the pot.
- Add two teaspoons of dried chilli flakes to the broth for bite.
- Bok choy cut into quarters is great. When the fish is almost cooked, add the chopped bok choy then cover for one minute or until it wilts..
- Drizzle Tamari and sesame oil over the broth when ready to serve.

2 CUPS FRESH OR FROZEN PEAS

2 TBSP LIME JUICE

1 CUP RAW CASHEWS

1 TBSP MINT, CHOPPED

½–1 CUP VEGETABLE OR FISH STOCK

SEA SALT AND WHITE PEPPER

4 JEWFISH FILLETS OR CUTLETS

2 TBSP OLIVE OIL

1 CUP EACH SNOW PEA SPROUTS AND
MINT LEAVES

1 TSP OLIVE OIL

1 TSP LEMON JUICE

Jewfish *with* pea puree [df, gf]

This is such a pretty dish to serve friends and family and it is very nurturing to sit down to eat on your own. The bright green peas will definitely put a bounce in your step and the raw cashews provide a rich smoothness and slight nuttiness—there's a depth and complexity to this easy meal.

SERVES 4

Place peas, lime juice, cashews and mint in a blender and process until almost smooth. Slowly add some stock until you reach your desired consistency—something like hummus. Add seasoning to taste. Pour into a saucepan and gently heat.

Season the fish well then place under the grill for about 2 minutes on either side, or until the flesh comes apart when pierced with a knife. Toss the snow pea sprouts and mint leaves with the oil for 30 seconds then finish with lemon juice. To serve, pour about ¾ cup of the pea puree into four shallow bowls. Top with the fish, then garnish with the dressed greens.

Variations

- Organic chicken or turkey could be used instead of fish.
- Snapper fillets, or another white fish like barramundi or blue-eye trevalla may be used instead of jewfish.
- Add 180 grams of silken tofu to the puree for a thicker, creamier and protein-rich meal.
- Try the puree as a sauce over pasta, in a vegetable pie, or simply add a dollop on steamed vegetables.
- Add about 750 millilitres additional stock to the blender to make a simple pea and mint soup.

4 VINE-RIPENED TOMATOES, HALVED

4 TBSP OLIVE OIL

2 TBSP BALSAMIC VINEGAR

4 CLOVES GARLIC, SKIN ON AND SQUASHED

1 TSP EACH SEA SALT AND CRACKED PEPPER

16 SARDINE FILLETS

1 CUP SPELT, BESAN OR RICE FLOUR

1 CUP BASIL LEAVES

4 LARGE BALLS BOCCONCINI

EXTRA OLIVE OIL AND BALSAMIC VINEGAR

Sardine stacks

Fresh sardines are completely different to those you find in a can. They taste more of the sea and are not as overpoweringly fishy. I find it hard to eat the canned variety now, but the fresh—well I can eat them almost anytime. Sardines are incredibly high in zinc, calcium, protein and omega-3 fatty acids. They are a staple in a Greek diet, which is reputedly the healthiest in the world.

SERVES 4

Place tomatoes, cut side down on a baking tray. Mix together 2 tablespoons of olive oil with the balsamic vinegar, garlic and seasoning and sprinkle over the tomatoes. Slowly bake at 100°C (200°F) until the tomatoes are soft and brown with the juices oozing out, about 30 to 40 minutes. Remove from the oven and place on a platter.

Meanwhile, lightly dust the sardines with the flour. Fry sardines in a hot pan with the remaining 2 tablespoons olive oil—you may need to do this in two batches. Cook for about a minute on each side or until golden. Drain on absorbent paper and crack some pepper over them—they won't need any salt as they are naturally salty enough. Layer the sardines on top of the tomatoes, then place a basil leaf or two on top of the sardines, followed by some bocconcini. Drizzle with the extra olive oil and balsamic vinegar and add cracked pepper to finish.

Variations

- When coating the sardines, start with the flour, then dip the fish into beaten egg, then more flour or spelt breadcrumbs to finish off.
- Serve the sardines with a green salad and spelt sourdough toast instead of basil and cheese.

8–12 ZUCCHINIS

1 SMALL BLOCK SOFT TOFU

½ CUP QUINOA

1 CUP MIXED FRESH HERBS LIKE BASIL,
MINT AND PARSLEY, CHOPPED

1 GARLIC CLOVE, CHOPPED

SEA SALT AND PEPPER, TO TASTE

1 LITRE STOCK

1 TBSP ARAME (*optional*)

HANDFUL PARSLEY, ROUGHLY CHOPPED,
TO GARNISH

Stuffed zucchini [*df, gf, vg, v*]

Here's one from my mum's kitchen, with a twist. Traditionally you use lamb, white rice and garlic stewed in a tin of whole peeled tomatoes. This is my lighter, healthier, meat-free version. My body and tastebuds appreciate it and even my mum thinks these taste good.

SERVES 4

Top and tail the zucchini then take out the flesh, using either an apple corer or a small, long knife. Mash the tofu using a fork and mix with the quinoa, herbs, garlic and seasoning. Carefully fill the zucchinis with this mixture then lay in a pot, covering with the stock and arame, if using. Cover and steam until zucchinis are tender, about 20 minutes. Garnish with fresh herbs and serve with crunchy spelt sourdough bread.

Variations

- Use two fillets of finely chopped white fish instead of the tofu.
- Add half a cup of roughly chopped pine nuts to the stuffing mixture.
- Add two chopped tomatoes to the stock when simmering.
- In cooler months, place the zucchini in an oven dish with the stock and bake at 180°C for about 45 minutes instead of steaming.
- Add one teaspoon of sumac to the stuffing.

8 LARGE FIELD MUSHROOMS OR 16 MEDIUM BUTTON MUSHROOMS

1–2 TBSP OLIVE OIL

2 SPRING ONIONS, WHITE PARTS ONLY, CHOPPED

1–2 GARLIC CLOVES, CHOPPED

2–3 ANCHOVIES, CHOPPED (*optional*)

2 TBSP CORIANDER STEMS, FINELY CHOPPED

1 TOMATO, CHOPPED (*optional*)

1 CUP FETA OR SOFT TOFU, CRUMBLED

½ CUP HERBS LIKE MINT, BASIL, CORIANDER, PARSLEY, GREEN PART OF SPRING ONIONS, CHOPPED

Stuffed mushrooms [*gf*]

This is a really lovely recipe. The anchovies add a complex saltiness as they melt into the stuffing. I also love adding cooked quinoa, freekeh or brown rice to make it a more substantial meal. Feel free to add more vegies like corn, zucchini, beans, capsicum or carrots. Simply serve these wonderful mushies with a big handful of rocket dressed with a little good quality olive oil and sliced cucumbers or roast vegies and tahini dressing.

SERVES 4

Pull the stems off the mushrooms, chop the stems and put aside. Heat the oil in a flat pan, and add the spring onions, garlic, anchovies and coriander stems. Sauté until it smells nice and softens. Add the chopped mushroom stems and cook until they soften. Add the tomato and feta or tofu and gently heat and stir until it starts to melt. Stir the herbs through.

Lay the mushrooms on a baking tray and fill with the stuffing. Pack it in quite firmly. Bake in the oven at 200°C (400°F) for about 10 minutes, or until the mushrooms look cooked—when they are soft and juicy.

Variations

- Use one leek, white part only, finely sliced instead of the spring onions.
- You could easily add different vegetables like corn, zucchini, asparagus, carrots, etc.—simply chop and add to the pan with the mushroom stems.
- Add a cup of cooked brown rice and/or quinoa when sautéing for a more substantial meal.
- A drained can of tuna in olive oil or half a cup of flaked smoked trout fillets added to the stuffing before filling the mushrooms will provide more protein.
- Two teaspoons of shiro miso paste makes a richer filling. A tablespoon of pesto is also yummy.
- Little party quiches are easy to make with this filling by simply adding a couple of eggs and baking in greased muffin trays.

Spice blend

2 TBSP CUMIN SEEDS

1 TBSP CORIANDER SEEDS

½ TBSP BLACK PEPPERCORNS

1 TBSP SWEET PAPRIKA

1 TBSP GROUND GINGER

1 ONION, DICED

2 GARLIC CLOVES, CRUSHED

1–2 TBSP OLIVE OIL

1 KG (2 lb 2 oz) GREEN BEANS

1 TBSP TOMATO PASTE

2 CANS DICED OR WHOLE PEELED TOMATOES

1 BAY LEAF

1–2 TSP SEA SALT

Loobia [*df, gf, vg, v*]

This is a traditional Lebanese dish that most Middle Eastern families will be familiar with, but I've tweaked it a bit. It is one of those dishes that appears regularly on our dinner table. It's super easy and really tasty. The yummy spice blend will keep in a jar for months, so make extra and add to other dishes. Serve Loobia with rice and hummus.

SERVES 4

Prepare spice blend by pounding the cumin, coriander and peppercorns to a powder in a mortar with a pestle. Add the paprika and ginger.

Sauté the onion and garlic in a large saucepan with the oil until translucent, about 2 minutes. Then add 1 tablespoon of the spice blend and gently sauté until the ingredients start to stick to the pan. Meanwhile, top and tail the beans but leave whole. Add them to the pot with the rest of the ingredients—you may need to add a little water as well if it's too thick. Let simmer until the beans are soft, about 20 minutes. Check for seasoning.

Variations

- Cut beans into two-centimetre pieces or push them through a bean slicer.
- Add two teaspoons of allspice powder to the onion and leave out the spice mix.
- Use no spices.

½ ONION, DICED

1 CLOVE GARLIC, CRUSHED

1 TBSP OLIVE OIL

1 CUP MUSHROOMS, DICED

1 ZUCCHINI, GRATED AND SQUEEZED OF EXCESS LIQUID

4 FREE-RANGE EGGS

½ CUP FETA, ROUGHLY CHOPPED

½ CUP MIXED HERBS LIKE BASIL, PARSLEY OR CORIANDER

SEA SALT, CRACKED PEPPER OR SOY SAUCE, TO SEASON

GREEN SALAD, TO SERVE

Quick baby frittatas [gf, v]

I make these a lot. Almost any vegetables can go into these delectable little morsels. They're a great way to use up any less-than-fresh produce in the bottom of the fridge. Be creative with them. They freeze beautifully so you will have them on hand for lunches, picnics or emergency dinners.

MAKES 24

Heat the oil in a fying pan. Add the onion and garlic and sauté. Add the mushrooms and zucchini and sauté until soft. Allow mixture to cool slightly then add the eggs. Now add the rest of the ingredients to the pan and mix together. Spoon the mixture into the small, non-stick muffin cases. Bake at 180°C (350°F) for 10 to 15 minutes or until golden brown. Serve with green salad.

Variations

- These are yummy wrapped in mountain bread with hummus and rocket.
- Add a tablespoon of finely chopped coriander root with the onion.
- Add two teaspoons of grated ginger with the onion.
- For a hit of protein add a cup of drained tuna in oil, smoked trout, red salmon, soft or firm tofu or mashed legumes with the feta.
- Season with a tablespoon of miso paste or Tamari instead of the sea salt.

2 CUPS BUTTERNUT PUMPKIN, PEELED
AND CUT INTO 2-CM CHUNKS

½ CUP OLIVE OIL, PLUS EXTRA

1 TBSP GINGER, JULIENNED

1 CUP CASHEWS, TOASTED

½ CUP SHREDDED COCONUT, TOASTED

1 CUP CORIANDER LEAVES

Yellow curry dressing

2 TSP PENANG YELLOW CURRY PASTE

100 ML COCONUT MILK

150 ML LIME JUICE

1 TSP FISH SAUCE

Pumpkin *and* coconut salad [*df, gf*]

Coconut is one of the few plant sources of saturated fat, and this is what gives coconut its bad reputation. But recent research has shown just how good coconut is for heart health. The oil is great for our skin and digestive system as well. This salad has a big personality, and is wonderful on its own or as a side to a piece of grilled fish or organic chicken.

SERVES 4

Coat pumpkin in oil and roast on an oven tray at 200°C (400°F) for about 15 minutes or until golden and tender. Cool. Heat ginger in a little olive oil until crisp. Drain on absorbent paper and cool. Meanwhile, mix together all the dressing ingredients.

Combine pumpkin with cashews and coconut in a bowl and pour over dressing. Toss, and serve at room temperature, garnished with coriander leaves and crisped ginger.

Saltwater seafood will heat your body due the salt content, so include it in winter. Oily fish like sardines, salmon, herring and trout are more heating too. Freshwater seafood is more neutral, so enjoy anytime.

Sides and dressings

3–4 LARGE HANDFULS GREEN BEANS

½ RED ONION, HALVED AND FINELY SLICED

½–¾ CUP TAMARI ALMONDS (*see page 146*)

1 TSP SESAME OIL

1 TOMATO, SLICED INTO WEDGES (*optional*)

KECAP MANIS OR TAMARI, TO DRESS

Green bean *and* almond salad [*df, gf, vg, v*]

Almonds, according to the Hindu Ayurvedic diet, are the healthiest nuts to eat. They like them without the skin but I think it's a shame to miss out on the fibre. Don't add the tomatoes if you're prone to inflammatory reactions from solanine, the chemical alkaloid found in the nightshade family of plants, which includes white potato, eggplant, capsicum and chilli.

SERVES 4 AS A SIDE

Wash beans, top the ends and lightly steam or blanch, making sure they retain their crunch. Refresh in cold water to stop them from cooking on in their own heat. Put the cooled beans in a bowl with the remaining ingredients and stir gently. Drizzle over a little kecap manis to serve.

½ CUP QUINOA

½ CUP ORGANIC BROWN RICE

½ CUP FREEKAH

¼ CUP MILLET

5 CUPS WATER

1 STICK KOMBU

Mixed grains [df, vg, v]

Having grains already cooked in the fridge means you're much more likely to eat them. Add a spoonful to salads, wraps or as a side to your vegies and protein for lunch. You don't have to add the kombu, but it's a good way to include sea vegetables in your diet and to make the grains more digestible. Eat these grains wherever you would normally eat white rice. These are likely to become a staple in your fridge. (Remember to eat cooked brown rice within 48 hours.)

MAKES ABOUT 3 CUPS

Wash the grains well, using a fine sieve to drain. Place grains and rice in a saucepan with the water and kombu. Bring to the boil then reduce to a simmer for about 15 minutes or until the water is almost absorbed and little volcano-like holes appear. Taste the rice, it should be almost cooked—if not, add some more water and continue simmering with the lid half on until it is. Turn the heat off, cover with the lid and let steam for another 5 minutes or so. Before serving, pull the kombu out, chop it up and put it back in.

Variations

- You could add two tablespoons of amaranth grains instead of or as well as the quinoa.
- Sprinkle the grains with Tamari Seeds (*see page 146*) for extra crunch.
- Throw in six dried, chopped shiitake mushrooms.

Corn and millet are drying grains so they are great in the cooler months to dry up phlegm and damp conditions like candida.

180 G (6 oz) FIRM TOFU

¼ CUP TAMARI

WATER, AS NEEDED

1 TBSP OLIVE OIL

½ CUP CAJUN SPICE BLEND/MIX

Cajun-spiced tofu [df, gf, vg, v]

I used to have this as part of a complex dish with a tomato salsa, buckwheat blinis and soy mayonnaise. All a bit too much for me these days, but I still make the Cajun tofu as it's really good. Use tofu as an alternative to meat-based proteins like chicken or meat.

MAKES ABOUT 12 TRIANGLES

Slice the tofu into 1-centimetre cubes, then slice diagonally to form triangles. Put it in a bowl or container with the Tamari and enough water to cover it. Cover and let it marinate in the fridge for at least an hour, or you can leave it for a couple of days.

Take tofu out of the marinade and pat dry with kitchen towel. Place the spices on a plate and press the tofu into it to coat. Pan-fry the tofu in a little olive oil in a heavy-based pan, or grill it. You may need to do this in batches.

Variation

- For a deep-fried tofu to add to stir-fries, curries, casseroles, salads or an antipasto plate, cut into 2-centimetre cubes and add a tablespoon of ginger slices to the marinade, leaving out the Cajun spices. Drain and deep fry in a wok with safflower or camelia oil.

1 TBSP ARAME, RE-HYDRATED

1 TBSP TAMARI

1 LEMON OR LIME, JUICED

1 TSP GINGER, GRATED

Steamed vegie dressing [df, gf, vg, v]

This is nice over steamed asparagus with Tamari Seeds (see page 146) as a garnish.

MAKES ½ CUP

Mix all the ingredients together.

1 TBSP OLIVE OIL

2 BUNCHES BOK CHOY, ENDS TRIMMED, QUARTERED

2 GARLIC CLOVES, CHOPPED

1 TBSP GINGER, GRATED OR JULIENNED

1 TBSP FISH SAUCE

1 TBSP TAMARI

1 TSP SESAME OIL

Asian greens [*df, gf*]

Leafy green vegetables are an essential part of our diet year-round. Gently cook greens in cooler months and eat raw in the warmer months. This is a dish you'll find yourself preparing frequently. I've suggested bok choy here, but you could easily use choy sum, tatsoi or Chinese broccoli instead. Any of these will be lovely served with brown rice, quinoa, wholegrain noodles or just on their own with grilled fish.

SERVES 4

Heat a skillet or wok over a high heat or flame. Add the olive oil and heat slightly. Toss in the greens with the garlic and ginger, and cook for one minute. Add the rest of the ingredients. Put the lid on, turn the heat off and let the greens wilt—be sure to keep them green and crunchy. Adjust flavours if necessary, and add more water and sauces if you like a wetter dish.

Variations

- Add a cup fresh shiitake mushrooms, chopped in half, with the oil, or half a cup of dried and sliced Chinese mushrooms, hydrated. Add the soaking liquid to the pan.
- Mix in a bunch of trimmed and halved broccolini with the bok choy.
- A sachet of dashi powder mixed in with the sauces makes these greens extra special.
- Garnish with a small, finely sliced bird's-eye chilli for extra zing.
- One or two tablespoons of kecap manis will make for a thicker, richer sauce.
- Garnish with Tamari seeds (*see page 146*).

2½ CUPS BROWN RICE FLOUR

1 CUP TOASTED SESAME SEEDS

½ CUP SESAME OIL

1½ CUPS BOILING WATER

2 TBSP TAMARI

1 BROWN ONION, SLICED

1 TSP OLIVE OIL

PINCH SEA SALT

2 CUPS PUMPKIN, THINLY SLICED, SKIN ON

2 TSP OLIVE OIL

1 TBSP MISO PASTE

CHIVES OR PARSLEY, TO GARNISH

Pumpkin *and* sesame tarts [*df, gf, vg, v*]

This pastry uses brown rice flour, which is much easier to digest than regular wheat grains. Brown rice flour has become increasingly popular not only because of its digestibility but because it's loaded with nutrients. These pastry cases are easy to make and are low in bad fat. The filling is limited only by your imagination, so go for it. Toss in vegetables, fish, prawns, tofu drizzled with pesto—whatever appeals.

MAKES ABOUT 20

Combine rice flour and sesame seeds in a bowl. Mix together the sesame oil, boiling water and Tamari and pour into the flour mix. Knead for a couple of minutes, then roll into a ball and allow it rest for 30 minutes under a dry cloth. Roll out the pastry with a little more flour to stop it from sticking. Using a pastry cutter or glass, create rounds to fit into individual muffin moulds. Bake at 200°C (400°F) for 15 minutes until golden—they will harden up once cooled.

For the filling, heat the oil in a pan. Add the onion and salt and slowly caramelise. Meanwhile, place the pumpkin and its seeds on a baking tray with the olive oil and bake at 180°C for about 15 minutes, until golden.

To assemble, scrape a dab of miso onto the bottom of each case, add a little caramelised onion, then top with a layer of pumpkin and seeds. Sprinkle chives or parsley over the tarts.

Variations

- Use natto miso instead of miso paste on the bases for a stronger flavor.
- Drizzle Tahini Dressing (*see page 149*) roughly over the top.
- For a different filling, quickly sauté half a sliced onion in a tablespoon of olive oil with one to two cloves of crushed garlic. When the onions change colour, toss in two cups of sliced mushrooms. Cook for a minute more and then add half a cup of crumbled feta and one tablespoon roughly chopped tarragon. Let feta melt slightly and season with cracked pepper.

3 SPRING ONIONS, WHITE AND GREEN PARTS SEPARATED, CHOPPED

1 TBSP OLIVE OIL

1 GARLIC CLOVE, CRUSHED

1 TBSP GINGER, GRATED

½ BUNCH CORIANDER, ROOTS AND LEAVES SEPARATED, FINELY CHOPPED

1 TBSP THAI YELLOW CURRY PASTE

1 TBSP WATER

½ CUP FIRM TOFU, DICED

1 CARROT, DICED

1 RED-SKINNED POTATO, DICED (*optional*)

1 TBSP FISH SAUCE

1 TBSP KECAP MANIS OR TAMARI

1 TSP SESAME OIL

1 CUP BEAN THREAD VERMICELLI, SOAKED, DRAINED AND CHOPPED (*optional*)

1 CUP PURPLE OR CHINESE CABBAGE, FINELY SHREDDED

1 PKT SMALL SPRING ROLL WRAPPERS (50 SHEETS)

Mini spring rolls [*df*]

Most of us enjoy a crisp spring roll. This recipe is lovely and includes only good oils. These spring rolls are not deep-fried and don't contain pork, so they automatically become a more contemporary and healthy choice. They're a great way to encourage your kids to eat more vegetables.

MAKES 25

Heat the oil in a pan and sauté the white parts of the spring onions with the garlic, ginger and coriander roots. Add the curry paste and keep stirring until the paste starts to stick to the pan. Add enough water to create a paste, then add the tofu, carrot and potato. Stir to coat. Add the sauces and sesame oil and simmer gently until the vegies are tender—about 2 minutes. Finally add the noodles, coriander leaves and cabbage. Stir well. Taste and adjust seasoning if necessary.

Peel all of the wrappers off individually and lay down crossed over each other so you have a pile of crisscrossed wrappers—this makes them easier to access, making the rolling process faster. Put a heaped teaspoon of mixture on each wrapper and roll up, tucking in the ends as you go. Wrap in a second wrapper to avoid breakage during cooking. Fry five rolls at a time in a non-stick pan with a small amount of oil. Drain and pile on a plate.

Variation

• Brush the spring rolls with a little oil and bake in a moderate oven until brown—about 15 minutes.

1–2 TBSP OLIVE OIL

1 WHITE ONION, FINELY DICED

2 CLOVES GARLIC, CRUSHED

½ CUP DRIED PORCINI MUSHROOMS

1 CUP FRESH SHIITAKE MUSHROOMS, FINELY CHOPPED

½ CUP ORGANIC, SHORT-GRAIN BROWN RICE

1½ LITRES GOOD VEGETABLE STOCK, SIMMERING

1 CUP HERBS LIKE BASIL AND PARSLEY, FINELY CHOPPED

½ TBSP SHIRO MISO OR 1 TSP SEA SALT

Mini risotto balls [df, gf, vg, v]

These make a filling, healthy and delicious party food. Risotto balls are a great way to use up leftover risotto, too. Feel free to use any vegetable you like if mushrooms aren't your thing. Try corn and crab; pumpkin; zucchini and mint or organic chicken.

MAKES ABOUT 25 BALLS

Heat the oil in a pan and add the onions and garlic. Sauté until the onions are soft and translucent. Meanwhile, soak the porcini mushrooms in enough hot water to cover them. When they have softened, drain and reserve the liquid. Add the porcinis to the pan with the shiitake mushrooms. Now, add the rice to the pan and stir to coat.

Add the porcini soaking liquid to the simmering stock. Pour the stock into the rice mixture one ladle at a time, stirring continuously. Be sure that all the liquid has been absorbed before adding the next ladle of liquid. Continue adding the stock until the rice is al dente. Remove from the heat and let the rice cool—this will happen faster if you stick a few metallic utensils in the mixture to let the heat escape. Stir through the herbs and half a tablespoon of the shiro miso paste or sea salt.

Using wet hands, roll a heaped teaspoon of risotto into a tight ball. Continue making the balls until the risotto is used up. Place the balls onto a well-oiled baking tray as you go. Bake for about 15 minutes at 180°C (350°F) until golden brown.

Variations

- Once the rice is al dente, add a cup of good quality cheese like Parmesan.
- Add a teaspoon of thyme leaves and two teaspoons of sea salt instead of miso.
- Make seafood balls by using chopped green prawns and flathead fillets. Add them with the last ladle of stock.
- Rather than making balls, serve as a risotto, adding more stock to make it wetter.
- Add ½ cup of white wine just after you've added the rice and coated it in the oil.

1 CUP ALMONDS
2 GARLIC CLOVES, CRUSHED

2-CM PIECE GINGER, GRATED
2 TBSP TAMARI

Tamari almonds [df, gf, vg, v]

You can buy Tamari almonds, but why would you when it's really easy to make them yourself? And they'll taste better and cost you less. Make them as you need them or, if you'd like them to last longer, leave out the garlic and ginger. Add them to your salads for a yummy crunch.

MAKES ABOUT 1 CUP

Bake almonds on an oven tray at 180°C for 10 minutes or until golden brown. Add the garlic, ginger and Tamari and stir well. Bake for another 5 minutes. Let cool and store.

1 CUP EACH SESAME SEEDS,
SUNFLOWER SEEDS AND PEPITAS

3 TBSP TAMARI

Tamari seeds [df, gf, vg, v]

I love these Tamari seeds and I'm sure you will too. When you feel like an extra something special added to your meal, try sprinkling these very yummy seeds over your salad or vegetables, in your wrap, or on top of a curry or casserole. They're high in zinc, calcium, protein and essential fatty acids, and are a really good way to get those good oils in your diet.

MAKES ABOUT 3 CUPS

Place all the seeds in a dry pan and pan-fry until golden brown. They cook quickly and can easily burn so shake pan regularly. Sprinkle over the Tamari and stir well. Let cool and store in an airtight container.

Variations
- Add half a cup of chopped macadamias to the mix.
- Some dried fruit like cranberries or sultanas will give you a lovely trail mix.
- If you'd like a topping for desserts or porridge, omit the Tamari.

1 CUP RAW CASHEWS

1 CUP SOY OR ALMOND MILK

¼ CUP CORIANDER STEMS, ROOTS AND LEAVES, CHOPPED

1 TBSP GINGER, CRUSHED

2 TSP FISH SAUCE

Cashew paste [df, gf]

While cashews are high in good fat, it's still fat, so be mindful to eat them sparingly. The good news though is that they're also packed with protein, calcium and complex carbohydrates. Use this paste as a spread on wraps or mix into stir-fried vegetables. Also try it as a condiment with fish.

MAKES ABOUT 1½ CUPS

Simmer the cashews in the milk for about 15 minutes. Cool a little then put into a food processor with coriander, ginger and fish sauce. Blend until smooth.

Variations

- Add a few tablespoons of chopped mint while blending.
- For a sweet paste leave out the coriander, ginger and fish sauce and add one tablespoon cocoa or Dutch cocoa powder and 1 tablespoon agave. And now it's vegan.
- Keep the nuts raw; blend them with the milk and add either the savory or sweet ingredients.

1–2 CLOVES GARLIC, CRUSHED
1 TSP SEA SALT
1 CUP HULLED TAHINI

½ CUP LEMON JUICE
WATER OR EXTRA LEMON JUICE
(*optional*)

Tahini dressing [*df, gf, vg, v*]

This dressing has become a staple in my fridge and I'm sure that once you taste it, there'll always be a jar ready for you to use in your fridge too. Tahini is simply ground sesame seeds, and you can buy it hulled or unhulled. It's very high in calcium and essential fats. This dressing gives you the creamy texture you might miss when you're avoiding dairy.

MAKES 1½ CUPS

Pound the garlic and salt in a mortar with a pestle or chop up finely. Mix it with the tahini and lemon juice, and refrigerate until you are ready to use it. You will find that the dressing becomes quite thick once it is chilled, so if you would like it thinner, add some water or more lemon juice to taste, to make the consistency like that of yoghurt. Season as you would like.

Variations

- Add a teaspoon of shiro miso paste, umeboshi paste, or grated ginger.
- Blend in a handful of coriander or basil leaves for green tahini.
- Omit the lemon juice and use umeboshi vinegar and a teaspoon of grated ginger instead.
- Mix tahini dressing with one teaspoon shiro or genami miso paste and use as a great spread on toast. Top the toast with poached eggs or sautéed mushrooms and loads of fresh herbs.
- Add ½ cup natural yoghurt for a creamier dressing.
- A pinch of cumin will add a Middle Eastern flavour.
- Add one teaspoon of ground white pepper if you like.
- Sprinkle a little paprika and olive oil over the top.

½ BLOCK TEMPEH

1 TBSP OLIVE OIL

2–3 TBSP TAMARI

Marinated tempeh [*df, gf, vg, v*]

Tempeh is a fermented soybean product, high in protein and easy to digest. It has a unique flavour though, and can take some getting used to. It contains B12, which is not easy to get if you're avoiding animal products. You can usually buy it in either a block or as flavoured patties. Serve with vegies, in a curry or stew, or eat as a snack.

SERVES 2 AS A SIDE

Slice tempeh into half-centimetre-thick fingers. Drizzle with Tamari and let it marinate for a few minutes. Pan-fry in the oil (or grill without the oil) until golden brown, then flip and brown the other side. Drain on absorbent paper.

Variation

- Add a teaspoon of grated ginger to the marinade.

1 CUP FRESH ORANGE JUICE

1 TSP TAMARI OR SHOYU

2 TBSP KUDZU

1 TBSP SWEETENER LIKE RAW HONEY, SPELT OR AGAVE SYRUP

1 TSP GINGER, GRATED

ZEST OF ½ ORANGE

1 SPRING ONION, FINELY CHOPPED

2 TBSP DRY SHERRY

SEA SALT AND CRACKED PEPPER

3 GARLIC CLOVES, CHOPPED

Orange *and* ginger sauce [*df, gf, vg, v*]

Two autumn flavours working beautifully together. You'll find this sauce transforms a simple fish or poultry dish or stir-fry into something quite special. Kudzu is related to arrowroot and is used to thicken sauces.

MAKES ABOUT 1 CUP

Heat orange juice in a pan over a low heat and add kudzu. Whisk until dissolved. Add the remaining ingredients and mix well. Serve immediately. For a thinner sauce, sieve before using it.

1 CUP RAW MACADAMIAS

1 BUNCH CORIANDER, WASHED WELL

½ CUP GOAT'S FETA

1 CLOVE GARLIC

1 TSP SEA SALT

1–2 CUPS OLIVE OIL

Macadamia pesto [gf, v]

Pesto has been enjoyed by many cultures and with good reason. There are a number of good oils in it. Using feta instead of the Parmesan makes it guilt-free.

MAKES ABOUT 1 CUP

Roast the nuts in the oven or dry pan-fry until golden—be careful they don't burn. Allow them to cool. Chop all of the coriander, including roots and stems and put in a mortar or blender. Add nuts, cheese, garlic, and salt and start pounding with the pestle or blitz. Add the oil slowly until you have a nice, wet paste.

Variations

- Use basil instead of coriander.
- Use pine nuts, walnuts or almonds instead of the macadamias.
- Leave out the feta.
- Add one cup grated parmesan instead of the feta.

1 TBSP OLIVE OIL

2 TBSP BROWN RICE VINEGAR

1 TSP RICE SYRUP OR RAW HONEY

1 TSP UMEBOSHI VINEGAR OR LEMON JUICE

Tangy digestive dressing [df, gf, vg, v]

There is nothing better than brown vinegar to aid digestion. Umeboshi vinegar has the added benefit of reducing acid in your body.

MAKES ¼ CUP

Whisk all ingredients together.

2 BEETROOT
½ CUP HULLED TAHINI
1–2 GARLIC CLOVES

2 LEMONS, JUICED
SEA SALT

Beetroot dip [*df, gf, vg, v*]

Many people eat only tinned beetroot, which has added sugar and salt. Fresh beetroot is easy to cook—either roast, steam or boil—and is a beautiful vegetable because of its colour and because it offers so much for good health. It's full of fibre, which assists your digestive system, and betacarotine for your skin and immune system.

MAKES ABOUT 2 CUPS

Boil the beetroot until it is soft. Run under the cold tap and rub the skin off. Place all the ingredients in a blender and blend until smooth. Taste and add a little more of whatever you like.

Variation

- Add a teaspoon of cumin powder to the mix for a Moroccan flavour.

½ CUP HULLED TAHINI
1 TSP UMEBOSHI VINEGAR
1 TBSP RICE SYRUP

1 GARLIC CLOVE, CRUSHED
1 TSP GINGER, GRATED
1 TSP TAMARI

Not peanut sauce [*df, gf, vg, v*]

This dressing tastes just like peanut sauce but is much better for you. The nutty flavour of the tahini combined with the tangy bite of the ginger brings it all together.

MAKES ABOUT 1 CUP

Mix all the ingredients together. It may become a little clotted; if so add a little water until you have the consistency of pouring cream.

⅓ CUP SHIRO MISO

½ TBSP MIRIN

1 LEMON OR LIME, JUICE AND ZEST

1 TSP GINGER, GRATED OR GINGER JUICE (SQUEEZED FROM GRATED GINGER) (*optional*)

Marinade for fish [*df, gf, vg, v*]

This delicious marinade is lovely on organic chicken as well.

MAKES ½ CUP

Mix all the ingredients together—you can thin it out if the consistency is too thick by adding more lemon or lime juice or water. When ready to use, rub over the fish and let marinade in the fridge for about an hour before you barbecue, pan-fry or grill.

Variation

- Add one teaspoon each lemon myrtle and pepperberry powder (an Australian bush spice).

½ CUP TAMARI

1 TBSP RICE SYRUP

1 TBSP GINGER JUICE (SQUEEZED FROM GRATED GINGER)

1 GARLIC CLOVE, CRUSHED

1 TBSP KUDZU, DISSOLVED IN ½ CUP WATER

1–2 TBSP LIME JUICE

Seafood dipping sauce [*df, gf, vg, v*]

This finishes off any fish or tofu dish wonderfully.

MAKES ABOUT ¾ CUP

In a small pan over low heat, mix together the Tamari, rice syrup, ginger juice and garlic. Then slowly trickle in the kudzu slurry, stirring as you go. Finish with the lime juice. Use it while it's still warm.

1 SMALL BLOCK FIRM TOFU, RINSED AND
CUT INTO THICK MATCHSTICKS

2 TBSP TAMARI

1 TSP SESAME OIL

WATER, AS NEEDED

Yummy tofu [*df, gf, vg, v*]

Tofu has a very subtle flavour and some people have told me they don't really understand the point of eating it. But it is one of those magic foods that lends itself to whatever you put it with, which is probably why strong Asian flavours work so well. Tofu has many wonderful properties, such as being a healthy vegetarian source of protein and amino acids. This tofu is good added to stir-fries, Fresh Spring Rolls (see page 16), Nori Rolls (see page 118) or a wrap for lunch. Once you try it I'm sure you will become a tofu lover.

MAKES ABOUT 2 CUPS

Place the tofu, Tamari and oil in a wok or non-stick or heavy-based pan. Add enough water to just cover the tofu. Bring to the boil then lower heat to a simmer. Continue to simmer until the liquid has absorbed, turning once. The tofu will turn dark brown.

Variation

*   Add a tablespoon of kecap manis for a thicker, sweeter and crunchier sauce.

Sweet things

---

6 EGG YOLKS, FREE-RANGE

1 TBSP COCONUT PALM SUGAR, GRATED

500 ML SOY OR ALMOND MILK

1 VANILLA POD, SPLIT AND SCRAPED

Soy custard [gf, v]

This is a simply lovely creamy custard. For chocoholics, I've been known to add half a cup of dark chocolate chunks to the milk, which I whisk in while it heats. To split and scrape the vanilla pod, see Black Rice Pudding (page 223).

SERVES 4

Place a stainless steel bowl over a saucepan of simmering water. Put the egg yolks and sugar in the bowl and whisk until they become fluffy. Meanwhile, have the milk heating in a separate pot with the vanilla pod and seeds. When the milk is warm, slowly add to the egg and sugar mix in a thin and steady stream, whisking while you pour. Be careful not to overheat the custard as the eggs will scramble.

Take off the heat when it thickens and reaches the right consistency. Strain the custard into a bowl to remove any clumps and the vanilla pod.

Variations

- Using almond milk will give you a hit of protein and calcium and make the custard much sweeter than using soy milk, so reduce the palm sugar to taste.
- Pour some of the custard into the bottom of the martini glasses and let set in the fridge, and finish with shaved dark chocolate.
- Use maple or agave syrup instead of palm sugar.

½ CUP FINE SEMOLINA (OR POLENTA)

2 CUPS SOY OR ALMOND MILK

2 TBSP PEAR OR APPLE JUICE
CONCENTRATE, OR AGAVE OR MAPLE
SYRUP (*optional*)

2 TBSP EACH LEMON AND ORANGE ZEST

1 CUP PASSIONFRUIT PULP

SMALL PATTY CASES

Passionfruit semolina cases
[df, gf, vg, v]

Semolina is highly valued in Ayurvedic cookery. It's part of the wheat family so eat sparingly if you're wheat sensitive. Corn and polenta dries up mucous in the cooler months.

MAKES ABOUT 24

Toast the semolina in a saucepan for a few minutes. In a separate pot gently bring the milk and 1 tablespoon of the sweetener of choice to a simmer. Slowly add the milk to the semolina, whisking constantly—it will get quite thick and start to bubble like volcanic lava. Turn down the heat and keep whisking for about 5 minutes.

Whisk in half of the zest. Let cool a little, then spoon a small amount into tiny muffin moulds lined with patty cases. Make them quite high and proud, putting a dent in the top of each one with your thumb or the back of a teaspoon. Bake at 180°C (350°F) for about 15 minutes until just changing colour. Let them cool a little, then refrigerate.

When ready to serve, place on a large platter and fill the dent with a little passionfruit pulp, then drizzle over the rest of the sweetener (if using) and finish with the remainder of the zest.

Variations

- Instead of individual cases, keep the semolina loose like a rice pudding and don't bake it—serve it in small bowls with the toppings instead. Or pour it onto a large platter garnished with the toppings and serve from the platter.
- Try adding nuts like slithered almonds, or pistachios, or macadamia pieces to the semolina.

½ CUP HAZELNUT BUTTER

2 TBSP RICE, MAPLE OR AGAVE SYRUP

2 TSP VANILLA EXTRACT

½ CUP HOT WATER

Hazelnut sauce [df, gf, vg, v]

This is excellent for pouring generously over the Crepes (see page 51) or the Fruit Compote (see page 219). It's so much better than the pre-packaged nut sauces. Try it over rice or soy ice-cream too, or add a big spoonful to a mug of warm almond milk and stir to combine—very soothing at night time.

MAKES ABOUT 1 CUP

In a small bowl combine the nut butter, syrup and vanilla extract. Slowly drizzle in the hot water, whisking until the sauce looks like rich gravy. OMG!

Store any remaining sauce, if there is any, in an airtight container in the fridge. It will last for weeks.

Variations

- Use any good nut butter—imagine how good macadamia or cashew nuts will taste—or the ABC (almond, brazil and cashew) nut combination.
- Heat a cup of any milk you like, for example rice, almond, goat or quinoa, and pour into your night-time mug with a tablespoon of this sauce.
- Add a tablespoon of the mixture to drinking chocolate.

Almond milk is high in calcium, protein, fibre and essential fatty acids. It's also high in price, but worth every cent.

1½ CUPS WHITE SPELT FLOUR

¾ CUP COCOA POWDER

½ TBSP BAKING POWDER, LOW ALLERGY

PINCH SALT

½ CUP ALMOND OR HAZELNUT MEAL

¾ CUP MAPLE SYRUP

½ CUP SAFFLOWER OIL

½ CUP COCONUT MILK

½ CUP SOY MILK

1 ORANGE, ZEST AND JUICE

Topping

1 CUP FRESH CHERRIES

¼ CUP APPLE JUICE, SUGAR FREE

½ TBSP KUDZU OR ARROWROOT

Icing

125 G (4 oz) DARK CHOCOLATE

175 G (6 oz) SILKEN TOFU

1 TBSP MAPLE SYRUP

3 TBSP FRESH ORANGE JUICE

Chocolate cherry friands [v]

Once you start using kudzu you'll wonder where it has been your whole life. It adds silkiness and thickens sauces beautifully. And it's great for your digestive tract. Make sure that the maple syrup you buy is the real one.

MAKES 12

Sift flour, cocoa, baking powder and salt, then add nut meal and stir to combine. In a separate bowl, whisk together maple syrup, oil, milk, orange zest and juice and whisk to combine. Pour mixture into greased friand (or muffin) trays and bake for about 15 minutes at 180°C (350°F) or until cooked when tested with a skewer. Allow to cool slightly before removing friands from the tray.

To make the cherry topping, remove stones from the cherries and place in a saucepan with the apple juice. Simmer for about 5 minutes—be careful not to let the cherries go mushy. Dissolve the kudzu in a little water or juice and add to the cherries. Stir for a minute until thickened.

To make the icing, melt the chocolate in a metal bowl over a saucepan of simmering water then place in a blender with the tofu, maple syrup and orange juice and process until smooth. Chill for at least 30 minutes.

To assemble, spread the chocolate icing over the friands and top with the cherry mixture.

Drinks

---

3 CUPS FILTERED WATER

4 TSP BLACK TEA LEAVES

3-4 STAR ANISE

1 TBSP GINGER, GRATED

8 CARDAMOM PODS

2 STICKS CINNAMON

8 WHOLE CLOVES

1 TSP BLACK PEPPERCORNS

2 CUPS ALMOND OR SOY MILK

4 TSP AGAVE OR RICE SYRUP

Chai tea [*df, gf, vg, v*]

There are many ways to make chai and each person will most likely say that their way is the best and most traditional way. Don't rush while making this tea. The time and effort you put into it is what you will get out of it. You may want to experiment a bit with the ratio of milk to water, and the amount of sweetener, not to mention the combination of spices you are partial to. This recipe is far from traditional. I like chai, but I'm not into white sugar and cow's milk, so this is a modified recipe. Start with about double the amount of liquid you want to finish up with.

SERVES 4

Place all the ingredients apart from the milk and sweetener in a pot on the stove. Bring to the boil then let simmer for 15 minutes. Add the milk and let simmer for another 5 minutes or so. Strain then serve in lovely little glasses or mugs. Serve the sweetener separately.

Variations

- Grind all the spices in a coffee grinder or lay them between two sheets of wax paper and run a rolling pin over them before adding it to the pot.
- You can grind up these spices and add a few tablespoons to flour before using in a cake or crepes.

2 TSP BANCHA TEA   2 SLICES GINGER
2 CUPS BOILING WATER

Bancha tea *with* ginger [df, gf, vg, v]

Bancha or 'third year' tea is made from the twigs of the green tea plant. It's very low in caffeine and contains a good amount of calcium and anti-oxidants. Bancha's lovely smoky flavour lends itself beautifully to fresh ginger, which is a wonderful aid to circulation. You can also use this tea where you would usually use black tea in teacakes and slices.

SERVES 2

In a teapot or individual Japanese cups with in-built strainers, pour the boiling water over the twigs and the ginger. Let infuse for a minute or two then serve.

Variations

- If following a macrobiotic diet, you could add an umeboshi plum to the tea to aid digestion.
- Sweeten with rice or agave syrup.

1 LITRE WATER
½ CUP GINGER, GRATED

½ CUP RAW OR MANUKA HONEY
½ CUP LEMON JUICE

Ginger nectar [df, gf, vg, v]

This is perfect when you've got a cold or a flu bug. The ginger will induce sweat, helping to expel toxins. The honey is antibacterial and the sour lemon juice aids the liver. In the warmer months let the nectar cool then serve with mint and mineral water for a refreshing elixir. Drink the nectar warm in the cooler months.

SERVES 4

Put the water into a large pot. Then, using your hands, squeeze the juice out of the grated ginger into the pot. Discard the flesh or save for when you make stock. Add the honey and lemon juice and let the nectar simmer until the honey has dissolved.

Variation

- Freeze into ice cubes and use in vodka and soda in summer.

Winter

The world is a big place and some areas just don't experience extreme winters, but that doesn't mean people in these areas can eat the same food all-year round. You need to *adjust your diet* according to how cold it gets in your region. If you live in a tropical zone you are unlikely to be craving lamb stew in winter. What you will be doing, however, is changing some things, like cooking your food a little more than you would in the very warm months of the year. So instead of *raw foods* you will be having *cooked meals*. Winter does have an effect on most places and it's good to take note of its influence on you.

Object

Winter is the season when you'll want to spend more time indoors. You tend to be contemplative, and want to eat hearty foods and go to bed a little earlier. The object in winter is to warm your internal body as the surface of your body cools down. It's time to rest and store energy, and it's important to keep warm.

Organ

The kidney and the bladder are the sensitive organs in winter. They look after your ears, bones, hair and the lower part of your body, including your sexual organs.

Emotion

This is the season when we all tend to feel a little more isolated, anxious and fearful. Many of us don't really enjoy taking a good, long hard look at ourselves and when we do, we often don't like what we see. I imagine this is part of the reason we don't stop and ponder our worlds often. But it is essential that you do for your wellbeing, and winter provides a near-perfect opportunity to reflect.

Symptoms

During winter you may experience problems with thinning hair and/or hair loss, weak knees, lower back pain and loose teeth. Your ears may be affected so you could have hearing loss, ear infections and tinnitus. Reproductive or sexual issues like urinary tract or kidney infections, impotence, sexual promiscuity or frigidity, frequent urination and/or incontinence are possible. It is a time when you undergo decreased growth of your body and mind in general.

Flavour & foods

- You don't want to dispel your energy in winter; it needs to be right there inside of you. This is made easier by eating slightly heavier foods.

- Salty foods take energy 'in and down', so including salty ingredients and condiments like miso, soy sauce, sea vegetables, sea salt, oysters, sardines, crabs, clams, millet and barley will help you look within.
- Add dark food to your diet—adzuki beans, seaweed, black beans, black sesame seeds, dark miso and soy sauce—as they are said to nourish and strengthen your kidneys.
- All legumes should be enjoyed now, especially the darker-coloured ones.
- Include fresh ginger to improve your circulation and look after your respiratory tract.
- Continue to use a little more good quality oil to help keep your skin moist.
- Dried foods, pickles and preserves are recommended at this time of year.
- All whole grains, especially millet and barley, are great now.
- Almond milk rather than rice milk is nice at this time of year as it is higher in good oil.
- This is the season to enjoy root vegetables, such as swede, kumera, red potato, turnip and parsnip.
- Parsley, tofu, wheat germ, kudzu and roasted nuts are also to be enjoyed in winter.
- Use herbs like rosehip, raspberry leaf, chicory root, aloe vera (gel) and burdock root.

Cooking methods

Cook your meals for longer over a lower heat, using more water and a little more quality salt and oil. Enjoy dishes like hearty soups and stews, casseroles and dahl. Also use your oven more. Roast your vegetables instead of stir-frying them. Bake your fish instead of steaming it.

Avoid

Avoid eating too much lamb, cinnamon, cloves, dried ginger and chillies. These are too heating, as are coffee, alcohol, marijuana and cigarettes. These substances cause us to lose body warmth. Also avoid raw and cold foods.

Fresh in winter

Fruit: apple / cumquat / custard apple / grapefruit / kiwifruit / lemon / mandarin / passionfruit / pear / persimmon / pomelo / quince / rhubarb / avocado / lime

Vegetables: bok choy / choy sum / beetroot / broccoli / Brussel sprout / cabbage / carrot / cauliflower / cavolo nero / celeriac / celery / fennel / garlic / ginger / horseradish / Jerusalem artichoke / kale / kohlrabi / leek / okra / olive / brown onion / parsnip / green pea / potato / pumpkin / shallot / silver beet / spinach / swede / sweet potato / turnip / witlof

Seafood: dusky flathead / deepwater flathead / grey mackerel / orange roughy / snapper / tailor / blue warehou / sand whiting / Pacific oysters / king prawns / crab

Breakfast

1 CUP AMARANTH

2 CUPS MILK LIKE ALMOND, SOY, RICE, OAT OR QUINOA

1 CUP WATER

1 TBSP COCONUT PALM SUGAR, AGAVE, MAPLE OR RICE SYRUP OR PEAR JUICE CONCENTRATE (*optional*)

1 TBSP PISTACHIOS, CHOPPED

Amaranth porridge [*df, gf, vg, v*]

This ancient cereal has been all but forgotten, which is a terrible shame as it's especially great for those who are gluten intolerant, iron deficient and generally malnourished. If you can't find amaranth on the shelves, ask your local health food store to order it in for you. Amaranth is particularly high in protein and iron and is a great cereal for babies. Cook amaranth the same way you would porridge made from oats. Soaking it overnight speeds up the cooking time (or use amaranth flakes) and roasting makes it more alkaline. Most of the food we eat is acidic and we need a balance of both.

SERVES 2

Soak the amaranth overnight. In the morning drain, then roast it in a heavy-based pan over a medium temperature.

In a separate pot bring the milk and water to an easy simmer then slowly pour it into the amaranth, stirring continuously. Keep stirring until the grains have softened. Taste, and if it's still a little crunchy then cook for a bit longer, stirring occasionally until the grains are soft. This will take around 5 minutes if you've soaked the grains overnight. If you're using the flakes, the cooking time will be only a couple of minutes. You may need to adjust the liquid, using either more milk or water. Lastly, drizzle over the sweetener, if using, and top with chopped pistachios.

Variations

- Add two tablespoons organic sultanas or other dried fruit instead of the sweetener.
- Two tablespoons of shredded or desiccated coconut will make your cereal richer.
- You could add slithered or chopped almonds or almond meal for a more intense nutty flavour, adding them just before the grain is cooked, or sprinkling over the top when serving.
- Top with stewed rhubarb in orange juice or Fruit Compote (*see page 219*).
- Use half the amount of amaranth and half quinoa grains.
- Sprinkle LSA over the porridge before serving.

8 ASPARAGUS SPEARS

8 GREEN PRAWNS

4 TBSP OLIVE OIL

4 GARLIC CLOVES, CRUSHED

2 TSP SEA SALT

4 SPRING ONIONS, CHOPPED

1 CUP GREEN BEANS, FINELY CHOPPED

4 CORN COBS, KERNELS REMOVED

1 TBSP TAMARI

2 TSP FISH SAUCE

½ CUP ITALIAN PARSLEY, CHOPPED

½ CUP BESAN (CHICKPEA) OR RICE FLOUR

SEA SALT AND PEPPER

4 FREE-RANGE EGGS

OLIVE OIL, EXTRA FOR FRYING

2 LIMES OR LEMONS, CUT INTO WEDGES, FOR GARNISH

EXTRA ITALIAN PARSLEY, CHOPPED, FOR GARNISH

Corn fritters *topped with* asparagus *and* prawns [*df, gf*]

Most of us love corn fritters when we go to cafés, but they're usually made with lots of white flour, butter and sour cream. This is my gluten-free version that I think tastes even better than the others. There's no need to limit these to breakfast, they are equally good for lunch, dinner or a substantial snack.

SERVES 4

Snap the woody ends off the asparagus and quickly steam or blanch in hot water with a little salt, but keep crunchy. Rinse under cold water to stop them cooking further.

Shell and clean the prawns, leaving the tails on. Stir-fry them in half of the oil, half the garlic and all the salt until cooked through, about 1 minute on each side. Set aside. In the same pan add the remaining oil and sauté the spring onions and remaining garlic. Add the beans and corn kernels and sauté for a minute. Next add the Tamari, fish sauce and parsley. Take off the heat and cool a little.

Mix together the flour and eggs with seasoning to taste. Transfer the vegie mix and prawns to a clean bowl and stir through the flour and eggs. Mix to combine. The mixture should be quite thick. In a clean pan, heat the extra oil for frying and pour in half-cup mounds of the batter for each fritter—you want the fritters to be quite thick, so cook them fairly slowly to prevent burning. Cook until brown, about 2 minutes, then flip and brown on the other side. Place fritters on absorbent paper then transfer to two serving plates.

Place two spears of asparagus in a cross on top of each fritter. Garnish with a tidy handful of Italian parsley and lemon or lime wedges. Finish with cracked pepper.

Variations

- For a simpler meal, leave out the asparagus and prawns and serve fritters with Salsa Verde (*see page 46*) or make the fritters smaller and serve under Pan-fried Fish (*see page 33*) with a dollop of Spring Salsa (*see page 44*).
- Another substitute for the prawns and asparagus could be an avocado, a cup of plain yoghurt and a tablespoon of lemon zest all mashed together.
- Add two teaspoons of ginger and two tablespoons of finely chopped coriander stems when you sauté the spring onions and garlic for the batter, and two tablespoons coriander leaves with the parsley.
- If don't wish to include the fish sauce and Tamari, use a little sea salt to season.

3 CUPS WATER

1–2 SACHETS DASHI

A FEW DROPS SESAME OIL

1–2 TSP TAMARI

1 SPRING ONION, WHITE AND GREEN PART SEPARATED, SLICED

180 G (6 oz) SILKEN TOFU

A FEW CORIANDER LEAVES

Silken tofu *in* Asian broth [*df, gf*]

I realise this may sound a little unusual, but I love starting my day with this particular dish—even in warmer months. It's quick and nourishing, so yummy, high in protein, low in fat and will keep your blood sugar happy for hours. What more could one want from brekkie? You'll love it, especially if you like a savoury start to your day.

SERVES 2

Put the water, dashi, sesame oil, Tamari and the white parts of the spring onion in a flat pan. Let it simmer for a minute while you prepare the tofu.

Silken tofu is quite delicate—not much more solid than custard. Use a knife to cut around the plastic top of the packet then remove the lid. Place your hand on top of the tofu and tip the container upside down—water will come out so you may want to do this over the sink—letting the contents fall into your hand and allowing the liquid to drain. Place the tofu on a chopping board and cut through the middle lengthwise, then into thirds width-ways, giving you six pieces. Place these carefully into your stock and let the tofu heat through.

Serve in bowls with a garnish of coriander leaves and the green part of the spring onion.

Variations

- You can use a lovely vegetable or organic meat/chicken stock instead of the dashi. In this case replace the water with the same amount of stock.
- A teaspoon of fish sauce added to the stock will make it even better.
- For a quick wake-up call, add a teaspoon of chilli flakes or powder to the broth.
- I almost always have this with either leftover organic brown rice and/or quinoa. Add about a cup before the tofu goes in.
- Make the broth and simply pour over cooked buckwheat or quinoa udon noodles, and garnish with grated ginger and sliced spring onions.

Lunch

---

1 HEAD GARLIC

6 ANCHOVIES

LOTS OF OLIVE OIL

1 EGGPLANT, SLICED LENGTHWISE

2 RED CAPSICUMS, DE-SEEDED
AND QUARTERED

2 ZUCCHINIS, SLICED LENGTHWISE

1 CUP BUTTON MUSHROOMS

2 TSP SEA SALT AND CRACKED PEPPER

½ CUP EACH ITALIAN PARSLEY AND
BASIL, ROUGHLY CHOPPED

Antipasto vegetables [*df, gf*]

For an extremely healthy and nourishing Mediterranean feast serve these vegies on a platter with pesto, hummus, lentils and toasted spelt sourdough. Make an extra quantity so you have these wonderful morsels on hand to add to wraps, salads or grain dishes whenever the craving arises.

SERVES 4 (OR 6 AS AN APPETISER)

Pound, blitz or chop the garlic with the anchovies, a little salt and enough olive oil to make a paste. Next, place all the vegies in a bowl and coat with the garlic paste, adding enough olive oil so that the vegies are fully coated. Check for seasoning. Place the vegies on an oiled chargrill (or on a tray in the oven) and cook over a high heat until they are getting soft. Flip and continue cooking until they are done. Finish with a sprinkling of herbs.

1 CUP EACH DRIED KIDNEY
AND BORLOTTI BEANS

1 ONION, SLICED

1 TBSP OLIVE OIL

1 TBSP EACH GROUND PAPRIKA, CHILLI,
GARAM MASALA, CUMIN
AND TURMERIC POWDER

½ CUP CORIANDER STEMS,
FINELY CHOPPED

1 CAN WHOLE PEELED TOMATOES

2 TBSP TOMATO PASTE

1 STICK KOMBU

1 LITRE WATER

1 TBSP SEA SALT

Spicy beans [df, gf, vg, v]

The dried spices in this dish will help to warm your body in winter and the beans will keep your blood sugar stable for hours and are high in fibre. It's a great dish to have in the fridge as it will last for days and is beautifully versatile. Try the beans in wraps with rocket, serve with brown rice and guacamole or with baked corn chips as a dip. Adjust the spices to your liking. And, as an added bonus, the beans will freeze nicely, so make lots.

SERVES 4

Sift through the dried beans to remove any stones or bits of grit. Soak overnight in plenty of water.

Sauté the onion in the oil until translucent, about 2 minutes. Add all the spices at once and stir. They'll start to stick, so add a tablespoon of water. Now add the drained beans, coriander stems, tomatoes, tomato paste and kombu. Add the water and bring to the boil, then lower to a simmer. Cook for about an hour or until the beans are soft. Keep topping up with water if needed. Season to taste.

Variation

- Use cumin seeds instead of powder.
- Add some fresh chilli or chilli flakes.

2 FREE-RANGE EGGS

2 CUPS ORGANIC BROWN RICE, COOKED THE DAY BEFORE

1 ONION, SLICED

2 TBSP OLIVE OIL

2 BUNCHES SILVERBEET

1 CUP FETA, CRUMBLED INTO BIG CHUNKS

½ CUP BLACK OLIVES, PITTED AND HALVED

1 TSP GROUND CINNAMON

CRACKED PEPPER

Brown rice spinach pie [*gf, v*]

There's no need to avoid eating pies just because you're avoiding wheat and pastry. Try this nutty and crunchy base made from brown rice. I've chosen spinach, feta and olives for this recipe but using the same sort of method, you could try any mix of fillings you like.

SERVES 4

Beat the eggs and mix into the rice. Press mixture into a 20-centimetre (8-inch) greased pie dish and bake until brown and crunchy, about 20 minutes. Set aside.

Meanwhile, using a wok, slowly caramelise the onions in the oil. Put in a large bowl. Wash and dry the silverbeet then, using a knife, take the leaves off the stalks and discard the stalks. Chop the leaves finely.

Add a little more oil to the wok and cook the silverbeet quickly in batches, allowing it to wilt lightly. It should still be green and a little raw. Put the silverbeet in the bowl with the onions and add the feta, olives, cinnamon and pepper. Mix well and taste for seasoning, or add some more feta if you wish. Spoon the mixture onto the pie crust and bake for about 15 to 20 minutes at 180°C (350°F). Let it rest for about 10 minutes before serving.

Variation

• Add half a cup of chopped parsley to the egg and rice mixture.

6 STICKS DRIED WAKAME
1 TSP GINGER, GRATED
2 TBSP LIGHT SOY SAUCE OR TAMARI

2 TBSP RICE WINE VINEGAR
A FEW DROPS SESAME OIL
2 TBSP TOASTED SESAME SEEDS

Wakame salad [*df, gf, vg, v*]

A seaweed salad is not something you see every day. These precious plants from the sea are so nutritionally valuable it's a shame not to include them in your diet. And this salad tastes great. Go on—be adventurous. Your thyroid will thank you for the hit of iodine.

SERVES 4 AS A SIDE

Simmer the wakame in a pot of water until soft—about 5 minutes. Reserve the liquid for stock. Drain any excess water out of the wakame then roughly chop it up into approximately 2-centimetre pieces. Combine the ginger, soy sauce, vinegar and sesame oil and pour over the wakame. Finish with a sprinkling of sesame seeds. This salad will last at least a week in the fridge.

Use Tamari or shoyu instead of mass-produced soy sauces that are full of bad salt and other additives.

1 DESIREE POTATO, SCRUBBED, CUT INTO WEDGES

1 RED ONION, PEELED AND QUARTERED

1 CUP SWEET POTATO, CUT INTO ROUGH CHUNKS

1 BULB FENNEL, QUARTERED

4 BABY BEETROOT, SCRUBBED CLEAN

1 ZUCCHINI, CHOPPED INTO 2-CM CHUNKS

1 CUP BUTTON MUSHROOMS

1 CORN COB, CUT INTO 4 PIECES

4 CLOVES GARLIC

FRESH ROSEMARY (*optional*)

EXTRA VIRGIN OLIVE OIL

SEA SALT AND PEPPER

½ CUP QUINOA

1 CUP WATER

2 TBSP TOASTED NUTS LIKE PINE, ALMONDS, WALNUTS

1 CUP HERBS LIKE PARSLEY, MINT, BASIL, CORIANDER, ROUGHLY CHOPPED

HANDFUL ROCKET OR BABY SPINACH

1 TBSP LEMON OR LIME ZEST

1 TBSP LEMON OR LIME JUICE

Roasted vegetable *and* grain salad [*df, gf, vg, v*]

A gorgeous way to get all the goodies you need in one dish. If you suffer from arthritis or diabetes it's better to leave the potato out as it's part of the nightshade family, which some people find gives them an inflammatory reaction.

SERVES 2

Combine vegies, garlic, rosemary and oil in a baking pan, season and mix well. Roast, turning once, at 200°C (400°F). After 10 minutes, remove the mushrooms, zucchini and corn as they don't take as long to cook. Continue cooking the rest of the vegies for another 20 to 30 minutes, until they are tender.

Meanwhile, wash the quinoa well and place in a saucepan with the water. Bring to the boil then lower the heat for about 5 minutes, until most of the water is absorbed. Put a lid on and turn the heat off. Let sit for at least another 5 minutes before taking the lid off (*see 'How to cook grains' on page 3*).

Combine the vegies, quinoa, nuts, herbs, rocket and zest. Squeeze over the juice and check seasoning to taste.

Variations

- Stir through a cup of flaked smoked trout.
- Use barley or organic brown rice instead of quinoa.
- Add a can of cannellini or navy beans or chickpeas to the salad when you mix it all together.
- Serve with Tahini Dressing (*see page 149*).
- Add a splash of umeboshi vinegar to finish.

2 CUPS WHITE SPELT FLOUR, SIFTED

¼ CUP OLIVE OIL

½ CUP FILTERED WATER

1 TSP SEA SALT

2 TBSP MACADAMIA PESTO (*see page 151*)

1 TOMATO, SLICED

OLIVE OIL, EXTRA

Pesto pizza [*df, v*]

You'll find this pizza easier to digest than a regular base because it uses spelt flour. And the macadamia pesto is a lovely change from the usual toppings.

SERVES 4

For the base, place the flour in a bowl and make a well in the centre. In a separate bowl mix the olive oil, water and sea salt together. Slowly pour this mixture into the dry ingredients and combine, using a fork. Don't over-mix. If the dough seems too sticky, then add a little more flour. Shape the dough into a ball, then a long log shape so that it will be easier to roll. Roll it out to about 1 centimetre thick—it is denser than your average pizza dough. Fit the dough onto a flat, oiled pizza tray.

To assemble, spread the pesto generously over the base, then top with a few slices of fresh tomato. Drizzle with a little olive oil and bake at 180°C (350°F) for 15 minutes. Serve with cracked pepper and a big green salad.

Variations

- Pizza topping can include chunks of feta, added before baking, or sliced bocconcini.
- Cover the base of the pizza with Napoli Sauce (*see page 180*) before adding the pesto, or layer with roasted pumpkin and goat's feta, dotting the pesto around the edges.
- Omit the oil for a lighter, crunchier base but add a little more water if you do.
- Lay a few anchovies over the pesto.

Napoli sauce

2–3 TBSP OLIVE OIL

1 ONION, DICED

2 GARLIC CLOVES, CRUSHED

2 X 400 G CANS CRUSHED TOMATOES

1 TBSP TOMATO PASTE

2 TSP SEA SALT

2 TSP CRACKED PEPPER

1 BAY LEAF

Ricotta sauce

2 CUPS FRESH RICOTTA

1 CUP SOY, RICE OR ALMOND MILK

1 CUP MACADAMIA PESTO (*see page 151*)

1 EGGPLANT, THINLY SLICED

2 CUPS JAP PUMPKIN, THINLY SLICED

4 ZUCCHINI, THINLY SLICED

½ CUP OLIVE OIL

2 TSP SEA SALT

CRACKED PEPPER

1 CUP MUSHROOMS, SLICED

1 CUP EACH ITALIAN PARSLEY AND BASIL, ROUGHLY CHOPPED

1 CLOVE GARLIC

PINCH SEA SALT

1 TSP OLIVE OIL

1 PKT SPELT LASAGNE SHEETS

180 G (6 oz) BLOCK FIRM TOFU (ORGANIC), THINLY SLICED

Lasagne [*v*]

It's difficult to dislike lasagne. The only real problem with it is that traditionally it contains wheat, dairy, yellow cheese and red meat, which is not necessarily good for you. After you try this recipe, you'll be hooked—it's a healthier version of a classic dish. I usually do a seafood version for Christmas Day lunch and often have my family wanting more and skipping the turkey.

SERVES 4-6

To make the Napoli, put the oil into a saucepan and heat. Then add the onion and garlic and cook gently for a minute or two. Add the tomatoes, tomato paste, salt and pepper and bay leaf. Cook for as long as you can but for at least 15 minutes and up to 30 minutes maximum.

To make the ricotta sauce, mix the ricotta, milk and pesto together. It should look like a soft lumpy sauce. Add a little water if it's too thick so that it is the consistency of cream.

Coat all the vegies in the garlic and oil and season. Place on an oven tray and bake for approximately 20 to 30 minutes on 180°C (350°F). You can chargrill them if you prefer.

Spread a little Napoli on the bottom of a rectangular 20 x 30-centimetre lasagne dish, then lay pasta sheets on top, covering the whole of the base. Spread enough Napoli over the sheets to cover. Add a layer of eggplant and sprinkle with fresh herbs. Next, do layers of pumpkin, ricotta sauce and a little cracked pepper. Top with more lasagna sheets followed by a layer of tofu, Napoli and more lasagne sheets again. Add layers of mushrooms, ricotta sauce and herbs, and crack over pepper. Next, another layer of lasagne sheets, Napoli and zucchini. Finish with layers of pasta and Napoli, then spread over the last of the ricotta sauce and a little cracked pepper.

Bake at 180°C (350°F) for approximately 40 minutes or until lasagne sheets are soft—test by piercing with a knife. Serve with roughly chopped herbs over the top.

Variations

- Top the dish with a sprinkling of walnuts for extra nutty flavour and protein.
- For seafood, replace vegies and tofu with your favourite fish or other seafood. Rub the seafood in a paste of six crushed garlic cloves and six anchovies with ¼ cup olive oil.
- Cook two anchovies with the onion and garlic.

(see photo page 182)

4 BEETROOT

2 RED CAPSICUMS

2 RED ONIONS

2 TBSP BALSAMIC VINEGAR

2 TBSP MAPLE SYRUP, RAW HONEY OR AGAVE SYRUP

¼ CUP PEPITAS

Warm red salad [df, gf, vg, v]

The colour of this dish alone makes you want to eat it. It's a lovely winter salad, perfect to eat by itself or to accompany a roast dinner. Red vegetables are high in betacarotene, which our bodies convert to vitamin A. That's good news for the skin and immune system.

SERVES 4

Scrub the beetroot clean and cut it into quarters. Then quarter the capsicum and de-seed. Peel and quarter the onion. Place all the vegies in a baking dish and mix with the vinegar and sweetener. About 30 minutes into the cooking time sprinkle pepitas over the top and roast uncovered for another 10 minutes in a moderate oven, or until the beetroot is soft when pierced with a knife.

Variations

- Add a cup of lightly toasted pine nuts with the pepitas.
- Serve with some grilled or pan-fried haloumi, thinly sliced.
- Sprinkle over one teaspoon of freshly chopped oregano.

1 CUP PUY LENTILS, RINSED

2 TBSP EXTRA VIRGIN OLIVE OIL

1 ONION, DICED

2-3 CLOVES GARLIC, CRUSHED

2 TBSP CORIANDER STEMS, WASHED
AND FINELY CHOPPED

1 CARROT, DICED

2 STALKS CELERY, DICED

1 STICK KOMBU

1 BAY LEAF

FRESH OR DRIED THYME (*optional*)

500 ML FISH OR ANOTHER GOOD STOCK

SEA SALT AND PEPPER (*optional*)

2 TBSP FLAT PARSLEY, COARSELY
CHOPPED

DOLLOP YOGHURT (*optional*)

ONE LEMON, CUT INTO WEDGES

Lentil hot pot [*df, gf*]

I make this often in winter when it's cold outside and I want something easy to prepare. It cooks in just one pot and looks after itself, plus it's full of goodness. The lentils are a great source of protein that don't harm our environment like animal sources do (legumes don't create methane gas and don't need to be fed with chemicals). Make more than you need so you can have some for lunch the next day. Just add whatever vegetables you have in the fridge.

SERVES 4

Rinse and drain the lentils, soaking overnight if you can. Heat the oil in a large saucepan and cook onions over a low heat until soft. Then add the garlic, coriander, carrot and celery and stir until the veggies start to soften. Now turn up the heat and add the lentils and stir until all ingredients are coated in oil. Pour the stock in along with the kombu and herbs. (Do not add any salt now, as this will prevent the lentils from softening). Cook over a low heat until lentils are tender—about 30 minutes. You may need to add water. Season if necessary, then serve with parsley and yoghurt. Garnish with lemon. Nice with a scoop of quinoa and/or brown rice.

Variations

- Add pumpkin or sweet potato for a thicker hot pot.
- Diced zucchini is also a great addition.
- Add one teaspoon each of spices like turmeric, garam masala, cardamom and cinnamon for a Lentil Curry.
- Eat the next day with Tahini Dressing (*see page 149*) and baked corn chips.
- Add a handful of chopped kale with the stock.

Use lots of seaweeds as a garnish or ingredient.

1 TBSP OLIVE OIL

1 LEEK, WHITE PART ONLY, SLICED

1 TBSP GINGER, GRATED

½ BUNCH CORIANDER, STEMS
AND LEAVES CHOPPED SEPARATELY
(*optional*)

2 LITRES WATER

1 STICK KOMBU

2–3 SACHETS DASHI

4 DRIED SHIITAKE MUSHROOMS

½ CUP MISO PASTE

1 CUP SILKEN TOFU, CUBED

1 TSP SESAME OIL

2 TBSP SPRING ONIONS,
FINELY SLICED

½ SHEET NORI, SHREDDED (*optional*)

Winter miso soup [*df, gf*]

There is a miso soup in the summer recipes. While the winter and summer soups are similar, there are important seasonal variations, such as using fresh mushrooms in the summer months and dried in winter. Both are equally yummy and good for you.

SERVES 4

For the cooler months, start making the soup by sautéing leek, ginger and coriander stems in the olive oil until soft. Then add the water, kombu, dashi and mushrooms. Bring to the boil and simmer until the mushrooms are soft.

Remove the mushrooms and kombu and slice finely, discarding the stems of the mushrooms. Put the mushrooms back in the pot and turn off the heat. Stir through the miso paste, but do not boil—boiling kills the live enzymes in miso. To serve, divide the tofu between four bowls then pour over the broth. Drizzle over a few drops of sesame oil then finish with finely sliced spring onions, the reserved coriander leaves and the shredded nori, if using.

Variations

- Drop in two teaspoons of Tamari and one tablespoon of fish sauce when adding the miso paste.
- Serve over cooked organic brown rice, quinoa or quinoa noodles.
- Add noodles to the broth and let them cook while the broth is simmering.
- Put in lots of chopped vegies, like broccoli, cabbage, bok choy, fresh mushrooms, celery, carrots and/or beans before adding the miso paste and let it simmer until they're tender.
- A teaspoon of grated daikon makes a lovely garnish to this dish.
- Add a cup of diced firm tofu to the soup while cooking and omit the silken tofu.
- Use dashi without boneto (fish) flakes for a vegan miso.

When using dried shiitake mushrooms, remove their stems after softening and save them for making a stock at a later date.

2 TBSP OLIVE OIL

1 ONION, CHOPPED

3 CLOVES GARLIC, CRUSHED

1 TBSP GINGER, SLICED OR GRATED

2 STALKS LEMONGRASS,
WHITE PART ONLY, SQUASHED

1 TBSP CORIANDER STEMS, CHOPPED

1 TBSP GARAM MASALA

1 TBSP GROUND TURMERIC

1 TBSP GREEN CURRY PASTE

4 BIG HANDFULS JAP PUMPKIN, PEELED
AND CUT INTO SMALL CHUNKS

1 LITRE VEGIE OR FISH STOCK OR WATER

2 LIME LEAVES, FINELY SLICED

SEA SALT

DOLLOP OF GOOD YOGHURT, TO SERVE

HANDFUL CORIANDER LEAVES,
TO GARNISH

Thai pumpkin soup [df, gf, vg, v]

This is not your everyday pumpkin soup. It's rich, thick and fragrant. The onion, garlic and ginger are perfect ingredients to include now to keep winter colds and flus away.

SERVES 4

In a large pot, heat the oil and sauté the onion until soft. Add garlic, ginger, lemongrass and coriander stems and cook for a further minute. Now add the garam masala and turmeric and stir until it starts to stick to the bottom of the pan—you may need to add a dash of water at this point to prevent burning. Add the curry paste and cook until the paste is combined and heated through. Add the pumpkin and stir so the paste coats it. Pour in the stock (or water), lime leaves and salt. Bring to the boil and simmer until pumpkin is soft.

Remove lemongrass stalks and blend the soup. This soup is beautiful served with a dollop of yoghurt and garnished with the coriander leaves.

Variations

- Add a tablespoon of tamarind pulp to the stock for extra Thai flavour.
- Roast the pumpkin before adding to the pot—it will give the soup a richer taste.
- Garnish the soup with two garlic prawns in each bowl and then top with the coriander leaves.

3 SPRING ONIONS, WHITE AND GREEN PARTS SEPARATED, SLICED

1–2 TBSP OLIVE OR SUNFLOWER OIL

2–3 CLOVES GARLIC, CHOPPED

1 TBSP GINGER, GRATED

1 TBSP CORIANDER STEMS AND ROOTS, CHOPPED

4 CORN COBS, HUSKS REMOVED

1 LITRE VEGETABLE OR FISH STOCK

2 TSP FISH SAUCE

2 TSP TAMARI

1 TSP SESAME OIL

2 CUPS CRAB MEAT

1 TBSP KUDZU, DISSOLVED IN A LITTLE WARM WATER (*optional*)

2 FREE-RANGE EGGS, WHISKED

CORIANDER LEAVES

Sweet corn *and* crab soup [*df, gf*]

I remember ordering this soup as a kid whenever my family went to a Chinese restaurant in the 1970s. Afterwards, I felt kind of sick. I guess because of the MSG, the refined vegetable oils so often used then and the fatty chicken stock. So I set about inventing my own version and, believe me, you'll love this one as much as I do. It's so easy and tasty and is great served in little Asian bowls for a starter or as Sunday night comfort food.

SERVES 4

In a large soup pot sauté the white part of the spring onions in the oil along with the garlic, ginger and coriander stems and roots. Let everything go soft and fragrant. Take the kernels off the corn by standing the cob on its end and running a sharp knife down the cob. Add the kernels to the pot and stir a little. Now add the stock, fish sauce, Tamari and sesame oil and let simmer until the corn is soft.

Allow it to cool slightly, then pour half the soup in a blender or food processor and blend until fairly smooth. (Alternatively, leave all the soup in the pot and use a stick blender, being sure to leave it fairly chunky.) Place the mixture back in the pot, add the crab and gently stir. Put the pot back on a low heat. Combine the kudzu slurry and the eggs and whisk into the soup in a thin stream, stirring continuously and being careful not to scramble the eggs. Taste to see if you need more Tamari, fish sauce or sesame oil.

Serve in small Asian bowls and garnish with coriander leaves and the green tops of the spring onions.

Variations

- The kudzu does the same thing as cornflour—it thickens it up. You can use arrowroot powder instead of the kudzu, or arrowroot in a little warm water.
- Instead of stock, use one litre of water and three sachets of dashi.

2 SMALL PKTS VERMICELLI
RICE NOODLES

4 CUPS BUTTON MUSHROOMS

2 TBSP CORIANDER STEMS

1 TBSP GINGER, GRATED OR
FINELY CHOPPED

1–2 GARLIC CLOVES, CHOPPED

2 TBSP KECAP MANIS OR TAMARI

¼ CUP WATER

HANDFUL CORIANDER LEAVES, ROUGHLY
CHOPPED

Mushroom *and* rice noodle salad
[*df, gf, vg, v*]

*The ginger in this salad will help ease arthritic pain and indigestion and the rice noodles
ensure it is gluten-free.*

SERVES 4

Soak the rice noodles in hot water for 10 minutes, drain and
roughly chop. If some of the mushrooms are bigger than the
others, cut them in half so they are all about the same size.
Wash the coriander stems well then chop finely.

Place the mushrooms, coriander, ginger, garlic, sauce and water
in a large baking dish and stir to combine. Bake for about 20
minutes at 200°C (400°F) or until bubbly and the mushrooms
look soft and juicy.

Add the drained noodles, stir through the coriander leaves
and serve.

Variations

• Add a cup of shredded purple cabbage to the baking dish with
the mushrooms.
• Finish off the salad with a few tablespoons of shredded nori.
• Add a few more drops of sesame oil before serving.

Dinner

---

1 BLOCK TEMPEH

½ CUP TAMARI

WATER, AS NEEDED

2 RED POTATOES, UNPEELED

2 HANDFULS GREEN BEANS, TOPPED

2 CUPS CABBAGE, CUT INTO BIG SQUARES

2 CARROTS, SLICED IN HALF
LENGTHWAYS THEN ON THE DIAGONAL
INTO 2-CM PIECES

2 CUPS BEAN SPROUTS

OLIVE OR CAMELLIA OIL, TO FRY

2 CUPS PEANUT SAUCE (*see page 209*)

½ CUP SHREDDED COCONUT

1 LIME, CUT INTO WEDGES

Gado Gado *with* tempeh [*df, gf, vg, v*]

This is a traditional Indonesian dish. Don't eat lots of it if you're trying to lose a few kilos, have diabetes or have gallbladder issues because the peanut sauce is quite fatty. Coconut is known to reduce cholesterol and aid weight loss thanks to its medium-chain fatty acids. Still, both the peanuts and coconut have a good deal of (good) fat so indulge only occasionally and enjoy!

SERVES 4

Cut the tempeh into small triangles. Place them in a bowl with the Tamari and enough water to cover. Let marinate for as long as possible, but for at least 30 minutes.

Meanwhile, boil the potatoes whole then cool. Steam the beans, cabbage and carrots until only just tender. Slice the spuds into 1-centimetre rounds and place them on each of the four plates. Top these with the carrots, cabbage, then half the sprouts.

Heat the oil in a wok. Cook the tempeh in the oil until brown and crunchy. Drain on absorbent paper. Drizzle the vegetables with the peanut sauce then garnish with the coconut and tempeh. Serve with wedges of lime.

Variation

• You could grill the tempeh, rather than cooking in the oil.

6 THIN WEDGES OF JAP PUMPKIN, SKIN ON

2 TBSP OLIVE OIL

SEA SALT AND CRACKED PEPPER

1 ONION OR LEEK, SLICED

2 GARLIC CLOVES, CRUSHED

1 TSP THYME LEAVES, CHOPPED

½ CUP PITTED BLACK OLIVES, HALVED

1 SMALL CUP FETA, CRUMBLED

1 CUP MIXED HERBS LIKE PARSLEY AND BASIL, CHOPPED

10 FREE-RANGE EGGS

2 TSP DIJON MUSTARD

Frittata [*gf, v*]

Frittata is good anytime—for breakfast on toast, lunch with a salad and tahini dressing, or wrapped in flat bread, or for dinner with steamed vegies. It's so versatile I've even sliced it thinly for bruschetta as a yummy snack or starter. Try my variations below for different days or moods. Serve it at room temperature during the warmer months.

SERVES 4

Place the pumpkin on an oven tray and drizzle with olive oil. Season and pop in the oven to bake at 180°C (350°F) for about 15 minutes, or until golden. Meanwhile, slowly caramelise the onion in a heavy-based pan that can later go in the oven (cast iron is great), over a low heat with a little extra olive oil. This should take about 15 to 20 minutes and the onions will go a lovely dark colour and become very sweet. Add the garlic and thyme and let cook for a minute more.

Place the cooked pumpkin like bicycle spokes around the pan on top of the onion. Evenly dot the olives around the pan, in between the pumpkin. Top with the feta and sprinkle over the mixed herbs.

Whisk together the eggs and mustard and gently pour into the pan. Leave the pan on a low heat for a minute or so, so the bottom of the frittata cooks slightly. Then place it in a very slow oven 100°C (200°F) for about 40 minutes, or until the egg is set. Let it cool before slicing into wedges or thin slices.

Variations

- Instead of all egg, use a mix of half a cup of any type of milk with eight eggs.
- Add a tablespoon of pesto to your egg mixture or dot it between the pumpkin when you layer it in the pan.

1 TBSP OLIVE OIL

1 ONION, DICED

2 GARLIC CLOVES, CRUSHED

2 TSP GINGER, FINELY CHOPPED

1 TBSP CORIANDER STEM AND ROOT, FINELY CHOPPED

1 TSP CUMIN POWDER

1 TSP TURMERIC

1 TSP GARAM MASALA

2 TSP CHILLI POWDER OR FLAKES

1 POTATO, CUT INTO CHUNKS

1 CUP PUMPKIN, CUT INTO CHUNKS

2 CARROTS, CUT INTO HALF MOONS

1 LITRE VEGIE STOCK

1 KAFFIR LIME LEAF, SLICED (*optional*)

1 TBSP TAMARIND PASTE (*optional*)

TAMARI, TO TASTE

1 TSP FISH SAUCE OR SEA SALT, TO TASTE

½-1 CAN COCONUT MILK (*optional*)

2 TSP SESAME OIL

COOKED BROWN RICE, TO SERVE

THICK YOGHURT, TO SERVE

½ CUP CORIANDER LEAVES, TO SERVE

1 CUP BEAN SPROUTS, TO SERVE

Basic curry [*gf*]

Once you know how to get the flavours right with a curry, the variations are almost endless and it's such an easy and satisfying dish to make. It's also a nice way to include turmeric in your diet, which is important as this spice is now thought to reduce the risk of Alzheimer's disease developing by almost half. And just one serve of curry a week will do the trick. It's also anti-bacterial, antiseptic, estrogenic and has a good effect on the liver. Curries are better made the day before you serve them as the flavours have time to combine and the sauce will thicken up.

SERVES 4

Heat the oil in a large soup pot, then add the onion and cook until soft. Add the garlic, ginger and coriander stem and root. Sauté for another minute, then add the rest of the spices. Cook until the mixture starts to stick to the bottom of the pot—you may need to add a little (say, a teaspoon) water here to stop it from burning.

Toss in the vegies and sauté for a minute or so until all they are coated with the spice mix. Pour in the stock, along with the lime leaf and tamarind if you're using them. Let the curry simmer until the vegies are soft and liquid has reduced and thickened—you may need to add more water if it gets too thick. The longer you cook it the better, but allow at least 30 to 60 minutes. Taste for seasoning, using Tamari and fish sauce or salt.

Add the coconut milk, if using, near the end of the cooking process as there is no need to boil it—just let it simmer for a few minutes to be sure it's heated through. Add the sesame oil just before you take the curry off the heat.

Serve with brown rice and a dollop of thick yoghurt and top with coriander leaves and bean sprouts.

Variations

- Try using different vegetables like corn, cauliflower, green beans and peas—check what's in your refrigerator and needs using up.
- Add a can of chopped tomatoes when you add the stock.
- For a fish curry, cut up two large flathead fillets into big bite-sized pieces. Just before serving place them on top of the curry and put the lid on—the fish will cook in a minute or two. Do use fish sauce with this curry.
- For a vegan curry use vegetable stock and either throw in a can of lentils (or dried lentils soaked overnight, but remember to add kombu when cooking) or chickpeas.
- Stir through a good handful or two of baby spinach just before serving.
- A good squeeze of lemon juice added before serving compliments curries beautifully.
- Garnish with Tamari Seeds *(see page 146)*.
- Use fish stock instead of vegie stock.

Make enough soups and casseroles in the cooler months to last so you can freeze and reheat as needed.

1 ONION, FINELY DICED

2 TBSP OLIVE, CAMELLIA OR SAFFLOWER OIL

2 GARLIC CLOVES, CRUSHED

2 TSP GINGER, GRATED

½ CUP CELERY, DICED

1 TBSP EACH GROUND CUMIN, TURMERIC AND GARAM MASALA

1 CUP SPLIT BROWN OR YELLOW LENTILS OR MUNG DAHL

500 ML VEGETABLE STOCK

1 BAY LEAF

2 TSP SEA SALT, OR TO TASTE, OR TAMARI

1 CUP CORIANDER LEAVES, TO GARNISH

1 LEMON, QUARTERED, TO SERVE

Dahl [*df, gf, vg, v*]

If millions of Indians have been eating this dish for centuries, it must be good. And good it is. I've experimented with so many different versions, but I think this is the best. Whole lentils keep their shape, whereas split lentils dissolve, making for a 'mushy pea' consistency. High in protein and fibre, lentils are fat free and a good source of complex carbohydrates.

SERVES 4

In a large pot, sauté the onion in the oil until soft and translucent, about 2 minutes. Add the garlic, ginger and celery and cook gently for another minute. Add the spices and stir together. The spices will start to stick to the pot—this is good but you may need to add a little water to prevent them from burning. Stir the lentils through the spice mixture and then add the stock and a bay leaf to the pot. Bring to the boil then reduce to a simmer and cook for about 20 to 30 minutes or until the lentils are soft.

Season with the salt if needed and garnish with the coriander leaves. Serve with lemon wedges.

Variations

- Substitute the garlic and ginger with asafoetida powder.
- Use fresh grated turmeric and cumin seeds instead of ground cumin.
- Add clean mussels to the dahl when it's almost ready. Allow them to steam until they open fully.
- Include one or two kaffir lime leaves when cooking.
- Add lots more vegies like diced zucchini, carrot or pumpkin with the onions.
- Add one teaspoon fish sauce.

1 SMALL WHITE ONION, DICED

1 TBSP OLIVE OIL

1 CLOVE GARLIC, CRUSHED

1 TSP GINGER, GRATED

1 TBSP CORIANDER STEMS (*optional*)

1 CUP MILLET

½ CUP QUINOA

500 ML VEGETABLE STOCK

8 SHIITAKE MUSHROOMS, DICED

1 TBSP ARAME

1 CORN COB, KERNELS REMOVED

1 CUP SWEET POTATO, GRATED

2 TBSP EACH ITALIAN PARSLEY AND CORIANDER LEAVES, FINELY CHOPPED

BIG HANDFUL MIXED LEAVES

½ CUP EACH BLACK AND WHITE SESAME SEEDS

Ginger and tahini dressing

1 TBSP HULLED TAHINI

1 TSP GINGER JUICE
 (MADE BY SQUEEZING GRATED GINGER)

1 TSP UMEBOSHI VINEGAR

WATER, AS NEEDED

Japanese millet *and* quinoa balls [*df, gf, vg, v*]

I often hear from my patients that this is one of their favourite recipes. It is a dish to make when you're in the mood for something tasty, nutritious, nurturing and easy to prepare. And the balls will freeze well, which is very handy if you are in a hurry. Use whatever vegetables you like or have. The millet goes mushy and this will make the mixture easy to roll into balls and stay together.

MAKES ABOUT 8 BALLS

In a medium-sized pot, sauté the onion in the oil until translucent. Add the garlic, ginger and coriander stems and stir again to coat. Add the millet and quinoa and stir to coat the grains thoroughly. Next, add the stock, mushrooms, arame, corn kernels and sweet potato. Simmer for about 20 minutes or until the grains are tender and almost cooked.

Take the pan off the heat, put a lid on it and let the grains continue cooking in their own heat for at least 15 to 20 minutes. Take the lid off and allow the mixture to cool before covering again and leaving in the fridge overnight.

The next day, make the dressing by whisking all the ingredients together, using enough water to thin it out to the consistency of pouring cream. Set aside.

Stir the herbs into the millet mixture. Using your hands, roll about ¼ cup of the mixture into a ball and roll in either the black or white sesame seeds. Keep making the balls, rolling half in black and half in white sesame seeds and place them on an oiled baking tray. Bake at 200°C (400°F) for about 10 to 15 minutes, or until they start to change colour. Serve on a platter with some mixed leaves and the dressing on the side or drizzled over the top.

Variations

- Adding half a cup of split red lentils or mung dahl with the grains will add more protein and make the pilaf thicker.
- Add any vegie you like to the mixture—grated zucchini (squeeze the excess water out), diced carrot, pumpkin or celery, for example.
- Add two teaspoons of grated ginger with the onions, and a teaspoon of sesame oil.
- Add some chilli and ground turmeric for extra spice and colour.
- Garnish with Tamari Seeds (*see page 149*).
- Don't make into balls, just simply serve straight from the pot.

(see photo page 200)

Most people feel damp and sluggish in winter so we need to eat drying and cooling food like corn, millet, radish and pomegranate. But others feel dry and cold. In this case eat moist and warm foods like nuts, seeds and avocados.

2 SMALL BLOCKS OF FIRM TOFU

4 TBSP HATCHO MISO

2 TBSP TAHINI

2 TBSP WHITE MISO

2 TSP DULSE (SEA VEGETABLE
AVAILABLE IN FLAKES)

2 TSP SESAME OIL

1 TBSP MIRIN

1½ PKT MUGWORT SOBA NOODLES

4 ORANGES, ZEST ONLY

4 TBSP ORANGE JUICE

1 TBSP UMEBOSHI VINEGAR

2 TSP WHITE PEPPER

Paw paw salsa

1 GREEN PAW PAW (PAPAYA),
FINELY SHREDDED

1 TBSP RICE WINE VINEGAR

1 TBSP UMEBOSHI VINEGAR

2 KAFFIR LIME LEAVES, FINELY SLICED

2 LIMES, JUICE AND ZEST

2 LARGE CHILLIES, FINELY CHOPPED

1 CUP CORIANDER LEAVES

Baked miso tofu *with* paw paw salsa *and* noodles [df, gf, vg, v]

Tofu is so mild on its own that it appreciates being surrounded by strong ingredients to make it tasty. Baking it, as I have done, allows flavours to really penetrate. The saltiness of this dish and the way it is cooked make winter a perfect time to serve this for dinner, or even lunch.

SERVES 4

Cut each block of tofu in half and then cut into two triangles. Rub the tofu with the hatcho miso and let it marinate in the fridge overnight.

Combine the tahini, white miso, dulse, sesame oil and mirin and rub the mixture onto the tofu. Bake at 120°C (235°F) for around 30 minutes.

Cook the noodles in plenty of water until al dente, then cool. Stir through the zest, juice, vinegar and white pepper and set aside. Combine all the salsa ingredients together in a bowl.

To assemble, simply place some of the noodles on a plate then top with the cooled tofu and paw paw salsa. Yum.

Variations

- You can use a lighter white miso like shiro instead of the saltier hatcho miso.
- Instead of tofu, use fish fillets, such as barramundi, snapper, kingfish or mahi mahi.
- Try mango instead of paw paw in the salsa.
- Use any noodles you prefer—spelt, quinoa, kamut or buckwheat.

OLIVE OIL, ENOUGH TO DEEP FRY

ICE, ABOUT 1 CUP

½ LITRE WATER

2 CUPS RICE FLOUR

2 SMALL FILLETS FLATHEAD, MAHI MAHI, MULLOWAY OR OTHER THICK, WHITE FISH

8 GREEN PRAWNS, SHELLED WITH TAILS LEFT ON, DE-VEINED

8 OYSTERS

8 GREEN BEANS OR ASPARAGUS SPEARS, TRIMMED

8 MUSHROOMS

1 SWEET POTATO, SLICED INTO 8 ROUNDS ABOUT 2 MM THICK

½ CUP SOY MAYONNAISE

2 TSP WASABI PASTE

½ CUP PONZU (JAPANESE DIPPING SAUCE) OR TAMARI

Tempura seafood *and* vegetables [*df, gf*]

Deep-fried food is not always bad. If you use good quality oil (and use it only once), and eat these dishes in the cooler months, you don't have to avoid the deep fryer. Every time I make this recipe I wonder why I don't make it more often. It's fabulous for a dinner party, as it looks and tastes great. Prepare the vegies and seafood ahead of time, and then simply cook when you're ready to eat.

SERVES 4

Put enough oil in a wok for deep-frying and heat. Meanwhile, crush the ice and put it in a jug with the water. Put half the flour in a bowl and add the iced water slowly while whisking with a fork. The batter should be thin and a bit lumpy. Put the rest of flour in another bowl and rub the seafood and vegies in it to lightly coat them.

When the oil is hot, but not smoking, drop the flour-coated pieces individually into the batter, and then into the wok. Fry in batches, being careful not to crowd the wok. Cook until golden and crunchy, turning once. Drain on absorbent paper.

Mix together the mayonnaise and wasabi paste. Serve the tempura with ponzu and wasabi mayonnaise in separate dipping bowls.

Variations

- Use safflower or camellia oil instead of olive.
- Pound together two tablespoons of coarse sea salt and a tablespoon of lime zest, and serve with tempura instead of the ponzu and mayonnaise.

2 X 180 G (6 oz) BLOCKS SILKEN TOFU
1 CUP RICE FLOUR
1 TBSP SEA SALT
1 TBSP SZECHUAN PEPPER

500 ML OLIVE OR CAMELLIA OIL, FOR FRYING
LIGHT SOY SAUCE, TO SERVE

Salt *and* pepper silken tofu
[*df, gf, vg, v*]

Silken tofu is a little tricky to handle as it has a texture similar to custard so it tends to break apart easily—in the East they say that wearing red helps it to stay together! Either way it is worth the effort as it's a lovely morsel. Tofu is known to be of benefit to the stomach and spleen.
SERVES 4

Gently remove the tofu from the packet. To do this, hold over a sink and place your hand over the packet, letting the tofu fall into your palm and the water drain away. Then pop the tofu onto a cutting board. Slice it in half lengthwise, then into thirds width-ways.

Season the flour and gently dip each tofu piece into the flour, turning it so all the sides are coated. Using a flayed slotted spoon, place the tofu in a wok with heated oil. Let them fry until they are golden and float on the oil. Drain on absorbent paper and serve with soy sauce.

Sides and dressings

½ CUP TAMARI
1 TSP SESAME OIL
1 TBSP BROWN RICE VINEGAR
1 TBSP GINGER, GRATED

12–16 OYSTERS
ICE, CRUSHED
2 TBSP SPRING ONIONS, JULIENNED
½ CUP CORIANDER LEAVES

Oysters *with* Asian vinaigrette
[*df, gf*]

Oysters are exceptionally high in zinc, which aids the reproductive organs, skin and immune system. Eat lots of them if you are trying to fall pregnant, have compromised immunity, or low libido.

SERVES 4

Mix together the tamari, oil, vinegar and ginger. Arrange the oysters on a platter atop the ice. Spoon one teaspoon of the sauce into each oyster and garnish with spring onions and loads of fresh coriander.

Variations

- These oysters are also good steamed in a bamboo basket over simmering water. Place some wax paper in the basket and carefully lay the oysters and their topping on the paper. Put the lid on and steam them for about one minute.
- Add one teaspoon mirin to the dressing.
- Try one teaspoon shao shing wine in the dressing.

Nori sheets can be used like flat or Lebanese bread; simply use them to wrap some steamed vegies or salad, and drizzle over some tahini dressing and umeboshi paste. A scoop of brown rice is nice, too.

4 NORI SHEETS
½ TBSP OLIVE OIL
1 TSP SESAME OIL

½ CUP SESAME SEEDS
1 TBSP TAMARI

Nori chips [df, gf, vg, v]

Nori chips are so well worth making. Make double this amount, then you will have them on hand to add to any salad or meal. Nori, like other sea vegetables, is reputed to remove heavy metals from your body and dissolve phlegm.

MAKES ABOUT 4–5 CUPS

Place the nori sheets on an oven tray and bake at 200°C for ten minutes. Mix the remaining ingredients together then drizzle over the nori. Bake for another five minutes. Let cool then break up with your hands into corn chip-sized pieces.

1 SWEET POTATO, CUT INTO ROUGH CHUNKS
OLIVE OIL

SEA SALT AND CRACKED PEPPER

Sweet potato chips [df, gf, vg, v]

Sweet potatoes are a great alternative to white potatoes. They're lower in starch and higher in vitamin A. They won't send your blood sugar soaring or cause inflammation the way eating too many spuds will.

SERVES 2

Scrub the sweet potato clean and cut into small wedges. Parboil in salted water until just tender. Drain, and throw onto an oven tray with olive oil and salt and pepper. Toss to coat then bake for about 10 minutes in a moderate oven 180°C (350°F) or until golden brown.

Variation

• Use a vegetable peeler or mandolin to slice the sweet potato very thinly, then bake.

1 LARGE EGGPLANT

8 ANCHOVIES

8 CLOVES GARLIC

SEASONING, TO TASTE

2 TBSP PARSLEY, FINELY CHOPPED

1 TBSP LEMON JUICE

Eggplant caviar [*df, gf*]

This is a beautiful dip or spread to have in the fridge, and is great to accompany meat, fish or poultry, especially if they're barbecued. Eggplant is a member of the nightshade family, so limit your intake if you have an inflammatory condition like arthritis, asthma or eczema.

MAKES ABOUT 2 CUPS

With a sharp knife make eight incisions into the eggplant and poke a clove of garlic and an anchovy into each hole. Place on the barbecue, turning every so often until the eggplant has been chargrilled all over, or pop in the oven at 200°C (400°F) for 20 minutes or so, until soft. It will start to collapse into itself.

Slice open the eggplant with a knife—be careful as it will be very hot inside—and scrape out the pulp. Gently mix the pulp with a little seasoning, parsley, and lemon juice.

Variations

- Add a tablespoon of tahini when mixing everything together.
- Mix in a tablespoon of chopped mint with the parsley.

1 ONION, DICED

1 TBSP OLIVE OIL

2 CLOVES GARLIC, CRUSHED

1 TBSP GINGER, CHOPPED

1 STEM LEMONGRASS, BRUISED

1 TSP GROUND CUMIN

1 TSP GROUND TURMERIC

1 TSP GROUND PAPRIKA

1 TSP CHILLI POWDER

1 CUP CRUNCHY PEANUT BUTTER

2–3 CUPS WATER

1 KAFFIR LIME LEAF, FINELY SLICED

1 TBSP TAMARIND PASTE

1 TBSP KECAP MANIS

Peanut sauce [*df, gf, vg, v*]

Peanuts are technically a legume, not a nut, and if they are conventionally grown (not organic), they will be sprayed with poisons. Be sure to buy organic peanuts and eat them in moderation.

MAKES 2 CUPS

Sauté the onion in the oil until soft. Add the garlic, ginger and lemongrass and cook for another minute. Now add the spices and cook until they begin to stick, stirring frequently. Stir through the peanut butter and add the water, lime leaf and tamarind paste. Simmer gently for about 15 minutes. Add more water if needed as the sauce thickens to reach your desired consistency. Stir in the kecap manis and serve over vegies or with stir-fry.

Variation

- Add one teaspoon fish sauce with the water.

To remove the uncomfortable gas that usually accompanies legumes, add a stick of kombu (or asafoetida) to the pot when cooking.

2 CUPS VEGETABLE STOCK

1 TBSP GINGER JUICE (SQUEEZED FROM GRATED FRESH GINGER)

½ CUP FINE POLENTA

2 TSP SEA SALT

GRAPESEED OR OLIVE OIL, FOR FRYING

Polenta chips [*df, gf, vg, v*]

Polenta is made from ground cornmeal. It used to be considered peasant food but now can be found on gourmet menus, which is wonderful news for our taste buds and for those following a gluten-free diet. These chips are great with the Tempeh Burger (see page 78).

SERVES 2-4 AS A SIDE

Gently bring the stock and ginger juice to a simmer. Slowly pour in the polenta in a thin stream, whisking constantly. The mixture will get quite thick and start to bubble like volcanic lava. Add the salt and turn down the heat but keep whisking for about 5 minutes.

Pour the mixture into a greased tray—you want thick chips so make sure the polenta is a few centimetres (1 inch) high in the tray—and set in the fridge for about 30 minutes. Take out of the fridge and slice into fingers about a few centimetres (1 inch) wide and 5 centimetres (2 inches) long. Deep fry the chips in a wok until brown and crunchy, and then drain on absorbent paper.

Variations

- Start by sautéing a chopped onion with an anchovy in olive oil, then add the stock and polenta and cook as above.
- Stir through some pesto or chopped basil.
- Serve the polenta wet, like mashed potatoes. It is great with lentils.
- After refrigerating, cut into triangles for a change.
- Brush with olive oil and bake or grill instead of deep-frying.
- Simply serve with Napoli Sauce (*see page 180*) and goat's cheese.

1 ONION, DICED

2 GARLIC CLOVES, CRUSHED

SEA SALT

2 TBSP OLIVE OIL

1 TBSP THYME LEAVES

1 CUP MIXED HERBS LIKE PARSLEY, BASIL AND MINT

1 LEMON, ZEST ONLY

2 CUPS QUINOA, COOKED

VEGETABLES OF CHOICE LIKE ZUCCHINI, WINTER CHESTNUT PUMPKIN, CAPSICUM, TOMATOES

Vegie stuffing [df, gf, vg, v]

This is a great way to use up any leftover grains or vegies that are just past their best. You can freeze the mixture in small quantities and pull out just enough to fill zucchini, pumpkin, capsicum and tomatoes. Stuffed vegies are great on their own or served with Napoli Sauce (see page 180) or Tahini Dressing (see page 149).

MAKES ABOUT 3 CUPS STUFFING

Over a medium heat, sauté the onion, garlic and salt in the oil until translucent, about 5 minutes. Add the herbs, zest and quinoa and mix well. Check for seasoning.

To serve, partially bake the vegetables, make a hollow in each one (how you do this depends on the vegie you're using), and then fill with the mixture. Put them back into the oven to finish cooking.

Variations

- Add one cup toasted pine nuts to the stuffing.
- Adding shiitake or porcini mushrooms will give you a meatier, more intense flavour.
- Instead of quinoa try using spelt couscous, millet, amaranth or brown rice.
- Cook in a pot with Napoli Sauce (*see page 180*) in summer instead of baking.
- Add two anchovies with the garlic.

1 BLOCK TEMPEH
2 TBSP TAMARI

½ CUP SESAME SEEDS
2 TSP SESAME OIL

Tempeh *and* Tamari croutons
[df, gf, vg, v]

Tempeh has an unusual flavour and does take a bit of getting used to. It's high in useable protein and helpful in maintaining a healthy gut flora. Children like it and it's especially good for them as it's easy to digest thanks to the fermentation process it undergoes. Tempeh contains vitamin B12, making it a good choice for vegetarians. These croutons make a great accompaniment to your salads or vegies, or are nice as a side on their own.

MAKES ABOUT 2 CUPS

Cut the tempeh into 1-centimetre cubes. Place on a baking tray with the Tamari, seeds and oil. Using your hands or tongs, mix gently until tempeh is coated with the other ingredients. Bake in a moderate oven for about 15 minutes, or until brown and crunchy.

1 CUP ANCHOVIES
1 TBSP RED WINE VINEGAR
2 TSP THYME LEAVES
2 TBSP BASIL LEAVES, SHREDDED

1 TBSP DIJON MUSTARD
½ CUP EXTRA VIRGIN OLIVE OIL
1 TSP CRACKED PEPPER

Anchoïade *[df, gf]*

Anchovies are very salty and have a strong flavour. They are also high in omega-3 oils, making them a good choice in reducing the risk of heart disease. This recipe is a little like a pate, so serve it on spelt or rye crackers, or with raw vegetables.

MAKES APPROX 1 CUP

Place all the ingredients in a food processor and blend until very smooth.
Taste and adjust flavours to your liking. Anchoïade will last in the fridge for months.

2 LARGE SWEET POTATOES, PEELED AND CHOPPED

1 TBSP GINGER, GRATED

⅓ CUP SOY, ALMOND OR RICE MILK

1 TSP SEA SALT

PINCH WHITE PEPPER

Sweet potato mash *with* ginger
[*df, gf, vg, v*]

This is a really lovely alternative to traditional mashed potatoes. The ginger will aid circulation in winter and help relieve pain associated with arthritis. You can also try this mash using cauliflower steamed until soft.

SERVES 4

Steam the potato with the ginger until tender. Mash with the milk and season to taste.

Variations

- Add a few drops of sesame oil.
- Try adding a handful of finely chopped coriander and/or mint leaves to the mash.

½ JAPANESE PUMPKIN, SKIN LEFT ON, CUT INTO WEDGES

1 CUP MAPLE SYRUP

½ CUP PEPITAS

Baked maple pumpkin [*df, gf, vg, v*]

This is a good way to get the kids to eat pumpkin. Adults, however, will need no convincing. This dish is very high in zinc, which is an essential mineral for skin, nails, hair, immune and reproductive systems and your digestion. Pepitas are the inside part of the pumpkin seed and will add a lovely crunch to every bite.

SERVES 4

Place the pumpkin on a baking tray and coat with the syrup. Bake in a moderate oven for about 15 minutes, then sprinkle over the pepitas. Bake for another 5 minutes or until golden brown.

1 CAN CHICKPEAS

½ CUP HULLED TAHINI

1 GARLIC CLOVE

½ CUP LEMON JUICE

2 TSP SEA SALT

Hummus [*df, gf, vg, v*]

Chickpeas are high in protein and vitamin C and low in fat, so hummus will keep your blood sugar stable and provide long-lasting energy. The tahini gives a dose of heart-healthy oil and the lemon juice is especially good for your liver. Use this fabulous spread in wraps, as a condiment or dip, or dollop a big spoonful on top of baked vegetables.

MAKES 2 CUPS

Drain the chickpeas and place them in a processor with the rest of the ingredients. Blitz until smooth. Taste and adjust the flavours as you like.

Variations

- Add one to two tablespoons of olive oil for a creamier hummus.
- Serve with a sprinkling of sweet paprika or turmeric.
- Add half a bunch of coriander leaves when processing.
- Add one teaspoon ground cumin to the processor.
- Blend the hummus with one cup of steamed, peeled Japanese pumpkin.

Sweet things

2 ORANGES
4 CUPS GROUND WALNUTS
1 CUP DUTCH COCOA POWDER
½ TSP CARDAMOM SEEDS,
FRESHLY GROUND

½ TSP SEA SALT
1 CUP MAPLE SYRUP
5 FREE-RANGE EGGS

Cocoa *and* walnut cake [*df, gf, v*]

Cocoa was once hailed as a chocolate replacement. It's not. It has very different qualities and taste. Use good Dutch cocoa for this recipe and you'll be very excited about having a gluten-, dairy- and sugar-free dessert.

SERVES 8

Boil the whole oranges in water until very soft, about an hour. Combine the dry ingredients in a bowl. In a food processor, blend the maple syrup and oranges to create an emulsion. Whisk the eggs to a foamy consistency in another bowl and fold through the maple syrup and orange mixture. Gently fold the wet ingredients into the dry and pour into a 20-centimetre greased and lined springform cake tin. Bake in a preheated oven at 180°C (350°F) for 45 to 50 minutes. Remove from the oven and cool completely before turning out.

Variation

- To make muffins instead of a cake, simply pour the mixture into greased muffin moulds and cook for about 20 minutes.

1 CUP ORGANIC BROWN RICE

3 CUPS SOY OR ALMOND MILK

2 TBSP ORANGE ZEST

1 ORANGE, JUICE AND PULP

1 APPLE, PEELED AND GRATED

½ CUP RAISINS

2 CARDAMOM PODS, SQUASHED

1 TSP GROUND CINNAMON

1 VANILLA POD, SPLIT AND SCRAPED

1 TSP ROSE WATER

½ CUP PISTACHIOS, ROUGHLY CHOPPED OR SLITHERED ALMONDS

¼ CUP PALM SUGAR, GRATED OR TO TASTE

Middle Eastern rice pudding
[df, gf, vg, v]

Mum used to make rice pudding for a quick dessert using white sugar, rice and milk. Looking back I'm sure she made it because it took one pan, was simple to make, and the ingredients were always sitting in the pantry. This is my version using whole grains and complex carbohydrates as sweeteners. It is also dairy- and sugar-free. It will take longer to cook than a more traditional rice pudding, but it's worth the wait.

SERVES 4

Put all the ingredients, apart from the sugar, in a saucepan. Bring to a slow boil then drop back to a simmer. Stir fairly constantly to prevent from sticking—or use a non-stick pan. It will take about 60 minutes for the rice to soften and you may need to add more water if it's getting too thick.

Add the sugar just before serving and stir in. Spoon into bowls or tall glasses.

Variations

- Garnish with a few nuts and orange zest when serving.
- In warmer months, chill before serving.
- You can bake this dish if you prefer—it will take at least an hour at 180°C.

2 NAVEL ORANGES

200 G (7 oz) SILKEN TOFU, DRAINED

250 G (9 oz) COCONUT PALM SUGAR,
GRATED, OR LESS TO TASTE

½ CUP CORN OR GRAPESEED OIL

400 G (14 oz) ALMOND MEAL

1 TSP BAKING POWDER (LOW ALLERGY)

Chocolate topping

1 BLOCK BELGIUM DARK CHOCOLATE

1 TBSP VEGETABLE OIL LIKE CANOLA
OR SUNFLOWER

Mini jaffa cakes [*gf, v*]

Dark chocolate is not something to avoid but like most things, eat it in moderation. It is high in antioxidants and has a great effect on the heart. Look for chocolate with over 70 per cent cocoa content.

MAKES 24

Boil the whole oranges in water until very soft, about an hour. Blend the oranges, tofu, sugar and oil until smooth. Combine the almond meal and baking powder and gently fold into the orange mixture—when combined it shouldn't be too sloppy. Pour the batter into little muffin moulds lined with patty cake cases and bake at 180°C (350°F) for 20 to 30 minutes. Let cool in the tray.

While the gorgeous little things are cooking, melt the chocolate and oil together in a stainless steel bowl sitting over a pot of simmering water. Give it a whisk to combine nicely. Dip the top of the cooled cakes into the chocolate and let set. Done!

Variations

- Instead of chocolate topping, try an orange syrup using 1 teaspoon of orange flower water, 2 cups of orange juice and 125 grams of grated palm sugar—put them in a pan and stir without boiling until the sugar is dissolved, then simmer for approximately 15 minutes until the syrup has thickened. While the cakes are still warm, brush them with a little of the syrup.
- Make a whole cake by baking in a greased and lined 20-centimetre cake tin at 180°C for approximately 30 to 40 minutes. Test with a skewer but it shouldn't be completely dry, so take care not to overcook the cake.
- Buy dairy-free dark chocolate to make this dessert vegan.

1 CUP DRIED APRICOTS

6 DATES, PITTED

½ CUP RAISINS

½ CUP DRIED CRANBERRIES

½ CUP UNSALTED PISTACHIOS KERNELS

1 CINNAMON STICK OR
2 TSP GROUND CINNAMON

½ TSP GROUND ALLSPICE

3 CLOVES

2 TSP GINGER, GRATED OR
2 TBSP DICED BUDERIM GINGER WITH
FRUCTOSE (NOT SUCROSE)

2 CUPS OF PEAR OR APPLE JUICE

Fruit compote [df, gf, vg, v]

Try this delicious fruit as a dessert or for breakfast with yoghurt or in a smoothie at any time of day. It's concentrated in natural sugar so be mindful not to overindulge. And definitely try to use organic dried fruit in this dish—it's better for you and tastes so much more flavoursome.

MAKES ABOUT 2 CUPS

Dice the apricots and dates and put them in a saucepan with all the other ingredients. Bring to the boil then drop to a simmer until the fruit is plump, soft and luscious, about 20 to 30 minutes. The fruit may soak up all the liquid, so watch it as it cooks and add more water or juice as needed. You want to aim for your fruit to be swimming in a good amount of syrup.

Variations

- Any dried fruit, provided it's organic, will work just as nicely or try a cup of fresh pears and apples, peeled and chopped.
- You can also use chopped or slithered almonds instead of or as well as the pistachios.
- Sprinkle with shredded fresh mint when serving.
- For extra zing, toss a tablespoon of lemon zest into the saucepan.

Dried fruit, unless organic, is usually dried with sulphur dioxide —a harmful chemical that affects the liver, hormone levels and the immune system — so buy organic or at least 'sulphur free'.

4 BOSC, D'ANJOU OR OTHER PEARS

1 CUP DARK GRAPE JUICE

1 CUP SUGAR-FREE APPLE JUICE

1 TBSP GINGER, GRATED

1 CINNAMON STICK

1 TSP GROUND ALLSPICE

4 TBSP FRUIT COMPOTE
(*see page 219*)

BUSH HONEY YOGHURT, TO SERVE

2 TBSP MINT, SHREDDED TO GARNISH

Baked pears *with* ginger *and* fruit compote [*gf, v*]

Preserved ginger is perfect to eat in winter as it will improve your circulation and digestion. Any kind of pear will be lovely—check what's in season in your area.

SERVES 4

Core the pears and peel just the lower half. In a baking dish combine the grape and apple juices, ginger, cinnamon and allspice. Place the pears in the pan with the liquid. Cover and bake for 25 minutes at 180°C (350°F) or until tender.

Remove from the oven and pour the liquid into a small saucepan. Simmer this syrup for about 10 minutes or until it has reduced and thickened. Meanwhile, fill the holes in each pear with a little Fruit Compote then place on individual serving plates or a large serving platter. Pour the hot liquid over and around the pears. Garnish with mint and serve with yoghurt.

Variations

- For an even lighter pear, omit the juices and simply steam the pears in a little water.
- Try mixing half a cup of almond butter to the Fruit Compote.

1 CUP WATER

250 G (9 oz) PALM SUGAR OR COCONUT
PALM SUGAR

½ TSP EACH CINNAMON, NUTMEG AND
CARDAMOM POWDER

2½ CUPS WHOLEWHEAT SPELT FLOUR

2 TSP EACH BAKING POWDER AND
BICARBONATE OF SODA

1 CUP CHOPPED WALNUTS

1 TBSP POPPY SEEDS

1 CUP PEPITAS

2 TBSP SUNFLOWER SEEDS

1 CUP EACH CARROT AND ZUCCHINI,
GRATED

180 G (6.5 oz) OMEGA SPREAD

300 G (10 oz) SILKEN TOFU

Vegan carrot *and* zucchini cake
[*df, vg, v*]

This is a great vegan recipe for muffins too. The tofu holds the cake together and is great to balance your blood sugar in the afternoon. It's a recipe full of goodness and taste. The mixture will freeze well too, so makes lots and cook as you need.

SERVES 12

Boil water, grate in the sugar and add the spices. Dissolve the sugar then allow to cool completely. Mix together the flour, bicarbonate soda, baking powder, walnuts and seeds. In a separate bowl combine the carrot, zucchini and Omega spread.

Beat the tofu with a whisk and add to the water mixture. Pour over the vegies and mix. Make a well in the centre of the flour mixture and pour in the vegie mixture. Gently stir to combine. Place in 25-centimetre non-stick, springform cake tin and bake at 180°C (350°F) for 40 to 50 minutes. You'll know it's cooked when you stick a skewer into the cake and it comes out clean.

Variation

- You can use any other flour in this recipe, as you wish.

1 CUP BLACK GLUTINOUS RICE, WASHED
3 OR 4 TIMES
¼ – ½ CUP PALM SUGAR, GRATED
1 VANILLA POD, SPLIT AND SCRAPED

2 CARDAMON PODS, CRUSHED
1 BAY LEAF
PINCH OF SEA SALT
COCONUT MILK, TO TASTE

Black rice pudding [*df, gf, vg, v*]

Warming, slow-cooked foods like this are perfect to eat in the cooler months of the year. This dish makes a lovely breakfast too. One of my favourites!

SERVES 4 TO 6 AS A DESSERT

Place the rice in a large saucepan and cover generously with water—about double the amount of rice. Split the vanilla pod down the middle using a small knife, keeping one end intact. Hold the attached end and scrape the seeds from the pod and put these into the pot. Toss in the pod in as well.

Add in all the other ingredients except for the coconut milk. Simmer until the rice is soft, about 30 minutes. If the rice is too thick, simply add a bit more water; if too thin, let it simmer longer. Increase sweetness at any time by adding more palm sugar, if desired.

Serve in nice little Asian bowls smothered in coconut milk.

Variations

- In the warmer months, serve chilled.
- Serve with berries or a mint leaf.
- Blend the coconut milk with a frozen banana.
- To make little dessert cups, pour into individual cups then simmer about a cup of coconut milk with a teaspoon of agar agar for about 10 minutes. Cool slightly then pour on top of each of the puddings and place them in the fridge to cool and set.

1 CUP PUFFED MILLET, QUINOA OR RICE

⅓ CUP SESAME SEEDS

⅓ CUP SUNFLOWER SEEDS

½ CUP DESICCATED COCONUT (*optional*)

1 CUP MIXED NUTS LIKE ALMONDS, CASHEWS, BRAZIL NUTS, HAZELNUTS, MACADAMIAS, UNSALTED, CHOPPED

1 CUP SULPHUR-FREE DRIED FRUIT, LIKE APRICOTS, APPLE, PEACHES, PEAR, CHOPPED

¾ CUP TAHINI

¾ CUP RICE SYRUP OR RAW HONEY

1 CUP EITHER SESAME SEEDS OR COCONUT, TO COAT

Bliss balls [*df, gf, vg, v*]

This is one of the first recipes I wrote, and it is still a favourite. I make these often as they'll last for months. I am always glad to see them in the pantry in the afternoon when I feel like something sweet. Leave out the nuts if you have allergies to them.

MAKES 24 BALLS

Place the seeds and nuts in a food processer and blitz, keeping it chunky. Put them into a bowl. Next, blitz the dried fruit and add to the seeds and nuts. Add the millet and coconut to the bowl and mix everything together with your hands. Put the mixture back into the food processor and gradually add the tahini and syrup while the motor is running. Taste the mixture and adjust the sweetness to your liking.

Using wet hands, take about 1 tablespoon of the mixture and roll into a ball, then coat in sesame seeds. Repeat until you've used all of the mixture. Store the balls in an airtight container.

Variations

- There are no set amounts for the ingredients so add more of what you like and less of what you don't, adjusting sweetness and consistency with tahini and rice syrup.
- Try adding half a cup of carob powder, Dutch cocoa, spirulina powder, LSA mix, oats or flaxseed oil.
- Add a few drops of rose or orange oil or essence.
- A cup of almond or hazelnut meal is a very yummy addition.

2 CUPS WALNUTS OR PECANS

½ CUP MAPLE SYRUP,
AGAVE SYRUP OR RAW HONEY

Maple walnuts [*df, gf, vg, v*]

According to Traditional Chinese Medicine, walnuts baked with honey are good for the kidneys, which is our most sensitive organ during this season. Feel free to use any sweetener like agave, honey or maple syrup in this wonderful recipe that is great served with yoghurt or rice or soy ice cream.

MAKES 2 CUPS

Put the nuts in a baking dish then pour the syrup over. Stir to coat all the nuts then bake in a moderate oven until fragrant and bubbling a little. This should take about 10 minutes.

Variation

• Sprinkle half a cup of dried cranberries into the mix.

Drinks

2 CUPS MILK, LIKE ALMOND, QUINOA, RICE, OAT, GOAT OR HAZELNUT

½ TABLESPOON AGAVE, RICE OR MAPLE SYRUP OR RAW HONEY

1½ TBSP GLUTEN-FREE DUTCH COCOA POWDER, NATURAL DRINKING CHOCOLATE OR COCOA POWDER

Warm chocolate milk [*df, gf, vg, v*]

The ritual of a hot milk before bed is comforting for most of us. It soothes us before sleep. Milk is high in tryptophan, as are figs, nuts and dates, and these actually do help induce sleep. But pasteurised and homogenised cow's milk, refined sugar and Milo aren't the healthiest things to be putting into your body, particularly in the evening, as their stimulating nature may keep you awake. Try these yummy alternatives. If you are sensitive to caffeine or have problems sleeping then avoid the cocoa powder and sweetener—just have warm milk or check out the variations below.

SERVES 2

Gently heat the milk in a pan on the stove. Add the sweetener and stir to dissolve. Pour a little of the milk mixture into your favourite mugs with the cocoa powder and stir to make a paste. Add half a cup more milk to your cup and then stir to mix in, slowly adding more milk as needed.

Variations

- Use half a tablespoon of nut butter instead of or with the cocoa powder.
- Try carob molasses (available from Lebanese grocery stores and some good delis) in your milk—you won't believe how good this is until you try it and molasses is a great source of iron.
- Sprinkle in a few saffron strands instead of the cocoa.

Glossary

Agar agar this is good to use instead of gelatine to set desserts. It is available in flakes, powder or bars and is sometimes called Kanten. Gluten-free.

Agave a complex sweetener from the cactus of the same name. It won't send blood sugar levels up and tastes like toffee. Gluten-free.

Amaranth one of the oldest cereal varieties cultivated, this was the principal foodstuff of the Incas and Aztecs. It is extraordinarily healthy as a cereal or foliage plant because of the high protein content—16 per cent—and its leaves are popular either as a vegetable or seasoning. Gluten-free.

Apple or pear juice concentrate a complex sweetener made from fruit. Comes as a thick syrup. Gluten-free.

Arame this seaweed contains ten times the calcium of milk and 500 times the iodine of shellfish. Keep in the fridge soaking in water and add it to salads or stir-fries as you need it, or add it as a dried ingredient to winter casseroles, grains and soups. Gluten-free.

Asafoetida this herb can be used to replace garlic and onions in most recipes. Gluten-free.

Bancha twigs off the green tea plant, bancha is anti-inflammatory, anti-oxidant and very high in calcium. Gluten-free.

Barley a whole grain high in nutrients, barley is recommended in the cooler months. It does contain gluten.

Besan flour made by grounding chickpeas. Gluten-free.

Bonito this is a type of tuna and is a key ingredient in dashi (see below). It is available in flakes and you can use it to flavour soups. Gluten-free.

Buckwheat this grain contains no gluten. It is nice roasted first, then steamed. It may strengthen digestion and improve circulation. Gluten-free.

Dashi a powdered stock that consists of shiitake mushrooms, kombu and bonito flakes. There is also a vegetarian option available without the bonito (fish). Gluten-free.

Dulse a seaweed rich in iodine and calcium. Use dulse in soups or as a condiment.

Freekeh made by roasting green wheat, this grain is easy to digest. Wheat, when harvested young, retains more of its proteins, vitamins and minerals and generates great health benefits. Use as you would any grain.

Kamut this is an unadulterated older cereal variety from ancient Egypt, and the grains are often three times the size of wheat. It is high in protein as well as being rich in amino acids and vitamins.

Kecap manis a sweet soy sauce that is available at Asian grocery stores. You'll also see it called *ABC sauce*. Gluten-free.

Kombu this seaweed contains 500 times the iodine of shellfish. It is also high in protein, iron and calcium. Use it in soups, salads, bean dishes and pickles and add kombu to lentils and grains or anything that you cook with water. Gluten-free.

Kudzu	related to arrowroot, kudzu is used to thicken sauces and to treat diarrhoea. Gluten-free.
Millet	the oldest cultivated variety of cereal in the world, this is an important basic foodstuff in Africa and Central Asia. It is rich in unsaturated fatty acids and vitamins. Gluten-free.
Mirin	this Japanese sherry is commonly used in sauces and stir-fries. Gluten-free.
Miso paste	a fermented soy product, miso is used in soups and sauces and is great for balancing gut flora and any other stomach complaints. Don't boil it as boiling kills the live enzymes it contains. Gluten-free.
Natto miso	this fermented soybean product is made from whole cooked soybeans inoculated with *bacillus subtilis*. It is high in protein, rich in fibre and has little sodium. Gluten-free.
Nori	a dried sea vegetable, nori comes in paper-like sheets. It can be eaten as a snack or wrapped around rice. It has the highest protein content and is the most easily digested of all the seaweeds. Garnish your vegetables or soups with shredded nori. Gluten-free.
Pepitas	the inside part of the pumpkin seed. High in zinc.
Polenta	made by grinding yellow or white cornmeal. Used in both savoury and sweet dishes. Gluten-free.
Quinoa	this plant grows in the Andes at altitudes in excess of 4000 metres, and its small seeds are rich in vitamins and nutrients. It's a seed from a herb rather than a grain, and was much prized by the Incas. Gluten-free.
Rice Syrup	a complex sweetener with the consistency of honey, but not as sweet. It is made by pounding brown rice. Gluten-free.
Semolina	the centre part of durum wheat obtained after processing and separating it. When mixed with flour it becomes couscous. It's used to make puddings and other desserts, pasta and breakfast cereals. Contains gluten.
Shoyu	a good quality soy sauce from Japan that contains wheat.
Spelt	an old variety of wheat originating in Persia, spelt contains gluten but is easily digested. It is high in protein and has immune-boosting properties.
Tahini	is made from crushed sesame seeds and is available hulled or unhulled. The former is used to make hummus. Gluten-free.
Tamari	this is the brand name of a good quality soy sauce from Japan that is wheat free.
Tempeh	a fermented soy product, tempeh is high in protein and easy to digest. Gluten-free.
Tofu	an unfermented soy product, this is high in protein and great for the spleen and stomach as well as for stabilising blood sugar. Gluten-free.
Umeboshi	these salted pickled plums have the effect of reducing acid in the body when eaten. The plums can be bought whole, and are also available as a vinegar or paste. Gluten-free.
Wakame	this has the strongest taste of the seaweeds. Use wakame as you would kombu or make into a salad. Gluten-free.

Index

Conversion tables

Please note that Australian spoon and cup measurements are used in this book.
All spoon and cup measurements are level, not heaped, unless otherwise indicated.

Temperatures

Gas Mark	Fahrenheit	Celsius	Description
¼	225	110	Very slow
½	250	130	Very slow
1	275	140	Slow
2	300	150	Slow
3	315/325	160/170	Very moderate
4	350	180	Moderate
5	375	190	Moderately hot
6	400	200	Moderately hot
7	425	220	Hot
8	450	230	Hot
9	475	240	Very hot

Liquid conversion

Metric	Imperial (approximation)
15 ml	½ fl oz
20 ml	⅔ fl oz
30 ml	1 fl oz
60 ml	2 fl oz
125 ml	4 fl oz
150 ml	5 fl oz
175 ml	6 fl oz
250 ml	8½ fl oz
300 ml	10 fl oz (½ pint UK)
375 ml	12½ fl oz
500 ml	17 fl oz
600 ml	20 fl oz (1 pint UK)
750 ml	25 fl oz
1000 ml (1 L)	33 fl oz

continued next page

Solid weight conversion

Metric	Imperial (approximation)
15 g	½ oz
20 g	⅔ oz
30 g	1 oz
60 g	2 oz
90 g	3 oz
100 g	3½ oz
120 g	4 oz
140 g	5 oz
170 g	6 oz
200 g	7 oz
250 g	9 oz
285 g	10 oz
300 g	10½ oz
375 g	13 oz
400 g	14 oz
455 g	16 oz
500 g (0.5 kg)	1 lb 1 oz
750 g	1⅔ lb
1000 g (1 kg)	2 lb 2 oz

International spoon and cup standards

	Australian	British	American
1 tsp	5 ml	5 ml	5 ml
1 tbsp	20 ml	15 ml	15 ml
¼ cup	60 ml	71 ml	59 ml
⅓ cup	80 ml	95 ml	79 ml
½ cup	125 ml	142 ml	119 ml
⅔ cup	160 ml	190 ml	158 ml
¾ cup	180 ml	213 ml	178 ml
1 cup	250 ml	284 ml	237 ml